Contents

Preface
A tough crowd   5

Introduction
Why I should have gone with the more dramatic title   10

Part One: The Preflight Briefing   **23**
1   Boy-ology: the three stages of the little man   25
2   What mums want   36
3   A curious paradox   41
4   My glass house and a handful of stones   48

Part Two: The Great Big Boy Debate   **55**
5   Is the sky really falling?   57
6   The boy brain: fact or fad?   62
7   It turns out Dad's not lazy; it's in his genes   69
8   Digging a little deeper into the 'boy brain'   72
9   The bit where I eat a slice of freshly baked
    humble pie   83
10 The crisis in boys' education – or is there?   86
11 Throwing like a girl: the gender similarities
    hypothesis   107

Part Three: Masculinity – On the Nature of Boys   **119**
12 Man stuff: masculinity in the new millennium   121

13 Personality: everything changes, and everything
    remains the same   128
14 Values maketh the man   141

Part Four: Raising Boys in the Real World   **159**
15 Communication: the language of boys   161
16 Lion-taming: managing boys' behaviour   176
17 Crime: when good boys go bad   184
18 Drop-kick dads   204
19 School   217
20 Extra-curricular activities   239
21 How to be a cool mum   257

Epilogue
    Trouble in Shoe-topia   265

Endnotes   269

Preface
A tough crowd

It's just before eight in the morning, and I'm the first act in a one-act play. I'm talking to 300 teenage boys, aged between 13 and 15, and their dads at the annual father-and-son breakfast at a boys' high school. I wasn't given much of a briefing, other than being told that I couldn't swear, and to try to make it entertaining.

The not-swearing bit made it a lot harder. If I'd been able to walk out on the stage and say something to the effect of 'Why do you guys start so *fucking* early?' I would have had them right there.

Instead, I'd have to rely on Plan B.

Sauntering into the hall, they look a bit like migrating buffalo coming down to the waterhole just after sunrise, blowing clouds of white smoke in the brisk morning air, full of noise and promise.

It's a tough crowd.

I recognise all the different types of boy. There's the popular boy, the trainee alpha male who's big, good-looking and surrounded by his copious mates. Then there's the wannabe cool guy, the guy who doesn't quite cut it and is too young to know that none of that stuff means anything anyway. There's the clown, the boy who's got a quick mind but who's yet to learn the value of stillness and the comforts of silence. Eventually, he'll realise these things are nothing to be afraid of, but for now they make him nervous so he fills them with crackle and pop. Then there are the fringe boys, the ones who don't fit the mould, the musicians, the school librarian types, the bookish kids with glasses and slender frames, none of them knowing that they're

5

much more likely to be the kings and king-makers. And dotted here and there are the free spirits: boys who don't want to play the stupid macho games of the herd. They're not popular and don't want to be. Bullies, too; I see one or two of them in the crowd with a couple of the inevitable henchmen in tow.

All of them are there; every shape and size you can imagine.

As they come in, they punch and shove each other, laughing and jostling and larking about as naturally as breathing. This is simply what boys do in large groups, and in small groups, too, for that matter. Elbows into ribs, and fists into shoulders, like an army band keeping the beat. None of the teachers even seem to notice the buzzing nonsense, or if they do they simply accept it for what it is.

Once the boys have settled, the head teacher stands up and a hush falls on the place with a well-practised grace. 'Good morning, boys,' he says, and I half-expect them to answer back but he pushes on. 'This year at the father-and-son breakfast we are lucky enough to have the pleasure of Mr Latta speaking to us.'

I feel a gazillion boy-eyes throw me a slightly disinterested gaze for a second or two before swinging back to the head teacher.

'Mr Latta is a psychologist who works a lot with young men and their families, and he has worked for many years with criminals as well. So, I'm sure you're going to find this a very interesting and very entertaining address. Without further ado, will you please welcome Mr Latta in the customary way.'

Three hundred boys start to clap and it sounds a little like a cross between the first roll of fresh thunder and a taunt. I told the head teacher to amp up the criminal stuff when he introduced me, because I thought that might at least pique their interest. I wish he'd amped it a little more. The fact that he'd said it was going to be interesting and entertaining was unfortunate as well. I'd been a schoolboy once myself and I'd had more than a few adults come in and talk at assemblies about various things. Usually they were pretty dull. If I'd been told by my head teacher that they were going to be entertaining, I would have switched off then and there, just to prove him wrong.

This is the point where you take a deep breath and jump.

'Right,' I say, striding out onto the stage. 'So who thinks their mums go on about stuff too much?'

They sit there, giving each other the *look*.

'Come on, you muppets,' I say. 'I'm not taking any names. I won't actually *tell* your mothers. Give me a show of hands: who thinks their mums go on about stuff too much?'

I swear to God that 95% of the hands in the room went up. I even saw some dads with their hands in the air.

'Right, now whose dad does stuff like hangs up the bathmat the way mum thinks it should be done?'

About 75% of the hands went up.

'And who thinks their dad gives in too easily to their mum, that their dad should put his foot down and tell her that he's not going to fold it the way she wants?'

About 95% put their hands up.

'OK, and who thinks that when you eventually grow up, and get married or live with some girl, that you're gonna tell her you're not gonna put the bathmat the way *she* wants, that you're gonna put it how *you* want?'

I watched what looked like 100% of those strong young hands thrust manfully up into the air.

Me and the rest of the dads laughed our arses off.

'Ah, my young princes,' I finally said, 'you guys have got a *lot* to learn about life.'

They didn't understand, but then how could they? These young men were just starting off on their own journey, and had yet to discover that eventually we *all* put the bathmat the way she wants. Not because we care about the mat, because we don't, and not because we think she's right, because we don't.

We do it simply because it's easier that way.

All kinds of trials and tribulations lay stretched out before these young men. Decisions both grand and trivial were scattered all along the way. Some of them they'd already begun to think about, and some they had no idea even existed. Some among them might go on to true greatness, and most would simply go on to live good lives. One or two of them might even end up in jail. Life is a complicated, perilous thing, yet somehow they would all eventually find their place in it. For some the road would be straight and well marked, and for others the road would be less travelled.

I love talking to groups like that, because the possibilities are so bright, you can't help but feel some hope for this tired old world we live in.

So I made them laugh for a bit, and told them funny stories about dumb criminals I've met in my travels. Then, when I judged that breakfast was becoming more of a focus than I was, I asked them a final question: 'How many of your mums get annoyed because you guys leave wee drops of pee on the toilet floor?'

No hands went up, but they laughed.

'You know what I mean, wee sticky drips you only find when you step on them?'

More laugher; no hands.

'Who thinks mums make too big a fuss about wee drips of pee?'

This time about 80% of the hands went up.

'So you think it's completely unreasonable for your mums to get annoyed about pee on the floor when there's a perfectly good toilet right beside it?'

The enthusiastic nodding they did was as clear an example of the difference between the worlds of boys and the worlds of mothers as you could ever hope to find. They really *don't* care about the little drips of pee. My hope is that by the end of this book, among a bunch of other things, you'll understand a little bit more about why that is.

You also might be pleased to know that I sent those youngsters away with this final thought:

Be nice to your mum, pick up your socks and make her cups of tea. She isn't going on about stuff – that's simply what good mothers do. Besides, she's the only one you'll ever have, so look after her.

Introduction

Why I should have gone with the more dramatic title

One of the best things in the world to be is a boy;
it requires no experience, but needs some practice
to be a good one.

Charles Dudley (1829–1900)

In many ways, the smart thing to do with this book would have been to buy into all the drama floating around out there about boys, because fear is the best motivator you can get to make people buy books. If I'd called the book *Boy Armageddon: How to Save Your Son From the Modern Plague That Wants to Destroy Him*, or *Why Boys are Falling, Failing and Flying Off the Handle and How to Make Them Happy and Perfect in Every Way*, or even *Boys: The New Lepers and How You Can Stop Their Bits Falling Off*, then a lot more people would have bought it. If I'd called this book *The Three Things You Need to Know to Stop Your Boy from Turning into a Drug Addict and a Criminal*, then I'd be on the *New York Times* Bestseller List.

I could do it, too; I could write that stuff, no problem. Here's an example of what the opening would have been like if I'd written that kind of book:

There has never been a time in human history when our boys have been in greater crisis. They fill our prisons, and on

Friday and Saturday nights their broken, bloodied bodies fill our hospitals and morgues. They are failing in schools in record numbers. They are trailing behind girls in all types of measures of academic performance and social adjustment. They are more at risk of using alcohol and drugs, more at risk of killing themselves and more at risk of both committing violence and being the victims of violence.

The numbers tell a bitter, frightening story of failure and growing despair.

What's more – and this is perhaps the thing that should fill us all with a cold dread – they are struggling emotionally as never before. In a world that increasingly values communication and the ability to express oneself as fundamentally important skills to survive in this hyper-connected, post-9/11 world, boys are isolated in a dysfunctional shell of sullen, angry silence.

Most of all, they are angry.

Abandoned by their fathers in record numbers, bereft of good male role models, given constant messages in the media which portray masculinity as toxic and bad and immersed in a world that is increasingly feminised, they retreat into an angry world of violent computer games, music that celebrates the denigration of women and drugs.

Then they retreat to their rooms with their rage, and their silence and snacks.

And all this is why so many of our boys are doing the unthinkable. All across the world, in record numbers, boys are burning ants with magnifying glasses. It isn't pretty, but it is an increasing reality for too many of our wounded boys.

It's been pretty tough for the ants as well.

So if we're going to prevent the wholesale slaughter of one of the natural world's most industrious of insects, then we have to learn how to reach out across this void of silence, and anger and snacks, and connect with them.

Obviously by this I mean connect with the angry, isolated boys. Connecting with ants seems a bit pointless because they probably don't have much to say that's of any real interest.

I mean, you know . . . they're ants.

Not bad, huh?

Even *I* started to get a bit worried for my own boys when I was reading that. Obviously the whole ant thing would need a little crafting to get some more impact, but given enough time and a few thousand words I could do it.

The problem is I just don't have the stomach for it. You see, I'm not entirely convinced by all the doom and gloom that seems to circulate around boys these days. There is no end of people queuing up to tell you that things are pretty dire so far as boys are concerned, and all of them are quoting neuroscientists and research psychologists and all manner of alarming 'facts'.

We're told that there's a crisis in boys' education, a crisis in boys' emotional lives, a crisis of male role models, a crisis of aggression, and drugs, and alcohol and hole-proof pants, and most of all a crisis in ant persecution.

Boys, apparently, are in crisis all over the place.

The problem is that boys as a whole don't seem to be terribly concerned about the fact that they're in crisis. They seem much more interested in dinosaurs, girls, exams or getting a job, depending on what stage they're at. I know there are some pretty dire statistics about boys, and we'll get to those a little later on, but it seems more like *some* boys rather than *all* boys are having problems.

Also – and I think this does lend me a certain degree of authority – I was a boy myself once, a little boy that is. Clearly

I'm not meaning to imply that I have recently made some major life choice and decided to live my life as Nigella. No, I mean that I experienced the whole boyhood thing, and I don't remember having much of a crisis about it at the time. One of the few crises I can recall revolved around the fact that my neighbour had a really cool Bionic Man action figure, (objectively I knew it was really a doll, but we called it an action figure, which made it OK) and I didn't. I really wanted a little plastic Steve Austin of my own, and it really ate me up for about a year or so. Apart from that, though, there didn't seem to be much in the way of crisis going around.

Yeah, yeah, you could say, but that was the '70s; things are different now.

Well, maybe, but I've got two boys myself and I've spent a bit of time involved in their lives. At time of writing, they're six and nine. My younger son actually *is* having a gender-based crisis: he doesn't like girls. No particular reason for that: he just doesn't. He's not mean to girls, and he actually plays with a few of the girls in his class, but when you ask him what he thinks about girls, he wrinkles his nose and says he doesn't like them.

Fair enough, I probably didn't like girls all that much when I was six, either.

I'm not too worried about that, because I'm pretty sure that he's going to re-assess the whole girl thing quite radically in a couple of years without any kind of intervention from me or his mother. Ironically, I think the next big gender issue he's going to face in the coming years will be too much girl-focus, not enough study-focus.

My older son, on the other hand, is a man of the new millennium. He doesn't have a misogynist bone in his body. One of his best friends is a girl, and they hang out quite a bit, which is nice. Actually – and this is the first tip of the book – it's a brilliant way to find out what's been going on at school. We ask him what's going on at school and we might get a little piece of information, but mostly we just get shrugs. Whenever his wee mate comes over, we ask her what's been going on at school and get a complete briefing of everything that's happened since we last spoke.

So tip one is this: When your boys are little, having a girl as a friend is very good because girls dish up all the dirt with very little prompting.

Still, I am just like everyone else: when I see some new story on the TV about how terribly boys are doing, it makes me worry for a moment or two as well. I see that boys are lagging behind in reading and writing, and I start to think, *Holy cow, what will become of my poor sons?* But then I see them writing stories at school, some of which are very funny, and I relax a little.

I see the stats about alcohol and drug use, and I fret. But then I have to contend with my younger son, who now won't listen to Jimi Hendrix because his mother told him Jimi used to take drugs.

I hear about all the statistics for boys and violence as I'm watching my own sweet little boy thump his older brother with a stick. But then I think to myself, *Well, fair enough because his brother was being really annoying.*

On top of all that, I've spent the better part of 20 years working with boys (and girls, too, by the way, but I'll leave that whole pile of chilli beans for the sequel). I've worked with little boys, middle-sized boys and big boys. In that time I've worked with lovely boys, and horrible boys and one or two really genuinely evil boys. I've also worked quite a lot with big boys who've done very bad things, including men who've killed people. I've seen both the best and the worst I think the world has to offer.

From time to time I've tried to estimate the number of kids and families I've seen, and each time it comes back as something ridiculous: varying amounts of thousands. Largely due to the shameful truth that I failed maths at university with an E (twice), I'm loath to trust my calculations, so let's just say it's a lot.

And here's the thing, while the surface stuff might have

changed over all that time, and the electronic stuff has certainly become way cooler, the boys themselves seem about the same as they've always been. I know we're all different, and unique and special, and all that syrupy nonsense, but we're also a lot more similar than we like to think as well. There are broad patterns that repeat over and over. I've certainly seen this stuff go round and round over the past two decades, but there's also pretty good evidence it's been going on for the past 2,000 decades.

The same old, same old

In Southern France there is a place called the Chauvet Cave, which contains something quite interesting. It seems that about 32,000 years ago a teenage boy crept in there and – using the Palaeolithic equivalent of a spray can (which in the good old days was tinted charcoal dust blown through a straw) — he made an imprint of his hand on the wall. It is the oldest known human image in existence. In fact there's an anthropologist called R Dale Guthrie who has determined on the basis of a detailed statistical analysis of the handprints that the majority of them were done by teenagers, and of those the vast majority were made by boys.

So, you see, they really have been messy souls from the very beginning.

No doubt shortly after that piece of graffiti went up 32,000 years ago there was also one of the earliest mother–son arguments in human history.

Cavemum would have come home from doing her shopping, seen that handprint and done her Palaeolithic nut.

'Who put this here?' she'd demand in angry tones, outraged that anyone could so senselessly deface her home. 'Well?'

Caveboy would pretend he hadn't heard her.

'I said who put this here?' she'd demand.

'I dunno,' he'd mutter, in an angry, sullen way.

'Well, it didn't just get there by itself, did it?'

He would have slumped into a surly, dejected heap at this point.

'I suppose you expect me to believe some *Tyrannosaurus rex* came in here and did it, then?'

Caveboy would have sneered at her. 'Jeez, Mum. This is the *Palaeolithic*, for God's sake. Dinosaurs haven't been around since the late Cretaceous. Don't you know *anything*?'

Unperturbed, Cavemum would have continued on: 'Do you have any idea how hard it is to keep this cave clean? Do you ever even think about that? I'm the only one that makes any kind of effort to keep this cave clean at all.'

Caveboy, knowing that there was no way to escape the oncoming lecture, would likely then have slumped as far down as he could.

Cavemum would have said a great deal more, but sadly none of that dialogue has survived in the fossil record. I think it would be a pretty safe bet, though, that pretty much the last thing she would have said would have been to lean in close to the handprint, dab it with one finger and then say, 'You know I'm never going to be able to get this out, don't you?'

Caveboy would have huffed something about how she was just overreacting and making a fuss.

She was right, though; she never did get it clean.

So why is it that mums and sons seem doomed to repeat the same arguments over and over and over? Why is it that, after 32,000 years of human evolution, with the invention of the wheel, and agriculture, and the written word, and the steam engine, and the industrial revolution, and the collapse of the Berlin wall, and finally electric toasters that have special settings for crumpets, he *still* thinks it's OK to make a mess all over the walls? And why is it that, after all that, when you try to point out that actually it's a pretty bloody unreasonable thing to do, he still acts like you're just making a fuss?

The thing is that while we might have flasher stuff, we still have the same brains as that caveboy and cavemum from 32,000 years ago. This might seem a little strange, because one would assume given that now we've got as far as electric toothbrushes and hair straighteners that underlying all that progress must be some pretty major changes in the human brain.

It just seems as if it must have got . . . well . . . *bigger* somehow.

Sadly, no. It's about the same size and shape as it's always been. Which means that all we've done so far has simply been to use the existing equipment in smarter ways. You could take a child born 32,000 years ago, raise him in our modern world and he would blend in seamlessly.

Weird, huh?

So while I'm sure that there have been a great many boys over the past 32,000 years who have been in one kind of crisis or another, the big picture seems to be that, at least at a general level, boys haven't given up just yet.

I'm not saying that boys don't have stuff going on, because they do, but it's been my experience so far that it's pretty much the same stuff they've always had going on. Like I said before, most of them seem far more interested in dinosaurs, girls or getting a job.

In truth, I think the only thing that's really new is the *drama* that we've built up around boys. Mums arguably sometimes find boys to be a bit of a mystery, and so tend to be more vulnerable to the anxiety produced by the drum-bangers and cymbal-clashers.

If your 11-year-old son suddenly stops talking to you and seems grumpy all the time, then, in my experience at least, mums are far more likely to believe that he's got some kind of underlying emotional issues than a more dad-orientated explanation, which is that he's just being a bit of a snot.

So then you go get a book, and if the book starts talking about 'the research' and going on about the 'crisis in boys' emotional lives', then you're going to start to worry after a paragraph or two.

I mean, there must be something pretty bad going on or else they wouldn't have gone to all the trouble of writing a book about it, right?

They've blinded us with 'science'

One of the things that surprised me the most when I got into researching this book in earnest, was how incredibly political the whole 'raising boys' thing has become. It soon became clear to me that it was really important to give mums (and whatever dads might also read the book) a better understanding about how much of the rhetoric around boys is driven by ideology and personal agendas rather than facts. I regularly found myself shaking my head in amazement as I read first the extravagant claims, and then the actual science these claims were supposedly based on. Time and time again it seemed that – even though it sounded like the claims being made about boys' brains, ears, eyes and all manner of other things were deeply rooted in rock-solid science – the truth was altogether flimsier.

'How can these people *say* this stuff?' I would mutter. 'How can you make a statement like that when the facts don't support it at all?'

It seemed to me that a lot of the people making the various claims were relying on the fact that no one was ever going to go back and check the references out for themselves, that we'd simply accept their interpretations of the research. Truthfully, most of us don't go and check stuff out for ourselves. Who has the time? We read in a book that 'the research shows blah de blah' and we just believe it.

Well, while I haven't gone and checked out every piece of research behind every claim that's ever been made about boys, I've seen enough to know that we *all* need to be a lot more cautious about the stuff we're being told about our boys. I didn't find anything that anyone just completely made up, but I did find example after example of claims that were gross exaggerations, blinding misinterpretations and some that were just plain wrong. We *all* need to understand more about the 'emerging science of boys', because important people are listening to some of these pop-neuroscience stories and making *real* policy decisions that affect *all* of our boys.

I've put a list of the more relevant papers and studies I've referred to at the back of the book so you can go check this stuff out if you want to. Wherever possible, I've put the online reference to make it easier for you to go look at it for yourself. I know most people won't, but if the urge should take you it's there to see.

So why this book?

I wrote this book because I wanted mums to know that they aren't bad for boys. I also wanted mums to be able to make more informed judgements about what does and does not matter for their boys, and to be more aware of the politics that underlie all parenting advice, *including* my own.

And especially the advice about boys.

While we're on the subject, my politics are simple, and fairly straightforward. I think that parenting has become far too complicated, and far too precious. We overthink just about everything when it comes to raising children these days. In particular, I think that the 'boy crisis' is getting a little out of hand. It might make a great story, and it's a great way to sell books, but I just don't think it's necessarily all that accurate, and I don't think that the 'boy crisis' is very relevant to the day-to-day business of raising boys. That's a much bigger political, scientific, philosophical debate.

You're not responsible for the world of boys, but you *are* responsible for *your* boy's world.

There is a subtle but incredibly important difference that I hope will become clearer as we go along.

The plan

So here's the plan. I'm going to spend the next four chapters giving you some of the important background stuff that will help you fit the rest of it together, and then we'll get into the really chunky bits:

Part I   Where we'll look at some of the fundamentals, mixed in with some context setting and a few other handy bits and pieces.

Part II   Where we'll have a closer look at the 'boy crisis' debate to see if things are really as bad as we're told they are.

Part III   Where we'll look at the whole masculinity thing, and more importantly three simple ways to teach your boy to be a good guy.

Part IV   Where we'll look at the practical side of raising boys in the real world. This where you'll find the nuts and bolts stuff.

As part of that process, we're going to look under the hood and take a peek inside the brains of boys. There are some very real questions that need to be asked about the *actual* differences between the male brain and the female brain. Once you step back from the pop-science interpretations of it all, there are some truly surprising things we've learnt about gender differences in brain functioning.

And I can pretty much guarantee that it's not going to be what you'd expect. You should probably warn your loved ones, friends and co-workers that you might get a little annoying during that chapter.

On top of all that, we're going to roam wildly and interestingly as we traverse the wide open spaces and twisty little canyons of boy-ness. It's a big sprawling landscape, and we're going to cover as much of it as we can. Communication is a big one for mums, so have no fear: we're going to cover off the fundamentals of 'boy talk'. I'm also going to give you loads of other practical stuff, too – stuff about education, feelings, girlfriends, role models, crime, cars, pocket knives, pizza and DVDs, building huts and computer games, to name but a few of the boxes of stuff we'll unpack. It's always good to come away from a trip with some practical things you can do to make your job a little easier once you get back to the real world.

For now, though, let me just say that if you read nothing more of this book, if you put it back on the shelf and go buy someone else's book, you should take away from our brief conversation this one, single, salient fact:

You missed some *really* good stuff.

Everyone else, follow me.

Part One

The Preflight Briefing

This is all the stuff you should know right at the start. If this was a plane, then this bit would be the equivalent of the wee talk they give you about the oxygen masks dropping in front of your face should you require 'additional oxygen' (what the hell is 'additional oxygen' anyway?), and the completely laughable 'brace position', which won't save your life but does mean that the air hostess doesn't have to watch you screaming all the way down.

I particularly like the bit where they say that if your life jacket doesn't fully inflate, you should simply blow through the tube to inflate it before leaving the aircraft. I have always wanted to ask what I should do if it hasn't fully inflated and my lips have been burnt away in the initial fireball after the plane hits the water at 600kph?

Also, how do I adjust the strap if I only have one arm left?

I never have asked that, out of consideration for anyone on the plane who might be scared of flying, but I always feel like asking.

This part of the book won't help you if you're in an actual plane crash either, although you could scribble a last message to your loved ones on it, I suppose. This is just stuff you should know at the beginning. This is the putting it all in a helpful context bit, and covering off the fundamentals right at the start. These are simply the things it helps to know before we take off.

1

Boy-ology:
the three stages of the little man

Three is a magic number. Almost everything comes in threes. There are, just as an example, three bones in the inner ear: the incus, malleous and stapes. There are even three types of colour receptors in the cone cells in your eyes – red, blue and yellow – just like the ink in your printer, except there it's called magenta, cyan and yellow. There are also, oddly, three parts to your bum: the *gluteus maximus*, *gluteus medius* and the lesser known but still highly prized *gluteus minimus*. It doesn't just end there, though, because all sorts of other things come in threes. Trilogies, for a start. *The Lord of the Rings* would have really sucked if it stopped just after Frodo was stung by the giant spider. The threes are endless – everything from little piggies, to billy goats gruff and blind mice. Musketeers also tend to come in threes, as do Powerpuff Girls, tenors, stooges, wise men and Dixie Chicks.

The three stages of boy-ology are no different. Obviously I've just made these stages up. You won't find them in any textbook or scientific thesis, but I find that they're a useful way to think about the broad developmental changes boys go through.

In keeping with the whole three-thing we've got going on, I'm not only going to describe my take on what those three stages are, but I'm also going to outline what I think the three key tasks for mums are at each of the three stages.

The other thing you might notice is that my first stage, Little Guys, actually begins at age two. This might cause you to wonder about what I did with the first two years. Nothing. Those years are still there, I didn't take them away; it's just that the first 24 months are pretty much the same for girls and boys, and they all need the same stuff: love, warmth, food, baby-talk and burping. Just do that for the first bit and you'll be fine.

Stage One: Little Guys
(2–6 years)
The bit where you introduce him to the world

Little Guys are fantastic fun. This is an amazingly magical time, because this is when you introduce him to the world. This is where he first meets things like cupboard doors, bars of soap, butterflies, shoes, chocolate, televisions, cardboard boxes, Sellotape, Spongebob Squarepants, toilets, monkeys, tricycles, wellies, girls, shells, feathers, pencils, school, rain, farting, bloody knees, sticking plasters, pulling off sticking plasters, lollies, toy cars, nose-picking, bedtime, birthday parties, Santa Claus, grandparents, goldfish, quiet time and the creepy lady who comes when you're asleep and takes your tooth from the glass or under your pillow and leaves you money.

All this stuff and an almost infinite amount more. This is when he first meets the world, when he first begins to discover what it's all about and what some of it means. Your part in this is enormous, because, while he will be at the centre of the universe, you will occupy a very significant position just to the right of centre. Whether you are with his dad, or by yourself, this is a time when his bond with you will be hugely important, because he will look to you to see what to think about things. He will follow your lead blindly.

As a result, the big three tasks with Little Guys are as follows.

1 *Provide a stable, secure, nurturing home.* This is all pretty straightforward, right? The stable, secure, nurturing home bit is important, because that's the stuff that kids need the most during these important early years. This doesn't mean you can never yell at them, because it's almost impossible to have children and not yell at them. In my house, just as an example, the thing I end up yelling the most is *'Would you guys STOP YELLING!'* So you don't have to be perfect, you just have to do the best you can. If your boy has some structure, some rules and he learns that the world (ie, you) behaves in a predictable way, then he'll have the best start that he possibly can.

2 *Start teaching him how to be a good man.* Don't worry too much about that now, because we're going to cover that off in Chapter 14. For now, all you need to be thinking about is that you start teaching boys how to be good guys when they're little guys. We'll get to the how later.

3 *Have as much fun as you possibly can.* This last point is at least as important as the first two. Little Guys really are fantastic fun. They're into superheroes and dinosaurs and all kinds of cool stuff. As a general rule, the more messy, loud and dangerous it is, the better.

If you're stuck about the kinds of things little boys like to do, I've included a list below of some of the sure-fire, must-do, have-to-do things for Little Guys.

◊ Building huts (inside with sheets, and outside with sticks and old bits of wood).
◊ Sleeping in the hut you built.
◊ Sleeping in a tent in the backyard.
◊ Jumping in puddles.

◇ Sliding down sand dunes.

◇ Poking about in rock pools at the beach.

◇ Throwing stones into rivers.

◇ Collecting bugs in plastic containers.

◇ Sword fights (if you don't have real swords, rolled up newspaper will do).

◇ Wrestling, rough and tumble.

◇ Being held upside-down.

◇ Being swung about by your feet.

◇ Forward rolls.

◇ Climbing trees.

◇ Falling out of trees.

◇ Walking along the tops of walls/fences with no one holding your hand.

◇ Running and yelling.

◇ Water fights (either with water guns or water balloons).

◇ Making farty noises with balloons.

◇ Popping balloons.

◇ Doing things that are a bit scary (usually these things involve height and/or speed).

◇ Toasting marshmallows (a real fire if you can make one, otherwise a candle will do at a pinch).

◇ Yelling — just yelling and yelling and yelling.

◇ Throwing paper darts.

◇ Going for a walk in the dark with a torch (and with you, of course).

◇ Playing outside in the backyard in the dark, with a torch, without mum.

◇ Reading *Where the Wild Things Are* at bedtime.

◇ Eating chocolate 'til you're sick.

◇ Kicking a ball about.

◇ Learning to ride a bike.

◇ Pizza and DVDs.

◇ Having friends over and running about like crazed little high-pitched savages.

◇ Getting dirty.

◇ Wearing holes in the knees of jeans.

◇ Acquiring all manner of cuts, bumps and bruises.

All these things are what make Little Guys such whopping good fun. It is a special time and should be cherished for the treasure that it is.

Stage Two: Big Guys
(7–11 years)
The bit where he gets to practise

This is the bit where he gets to practise the skills he's learnt so far. It's also the time to be developing and extending those skills even further. This brings with it new challenges and new joys. The challenges come from mastering your fear and letting him do things that make you more scared than him, and the joys come from watching him find his feet and push off deeper into the world again. This is a time when you begin to see the fledgling signs of who he will be really start to gain some purchase in the skin of the world. He will take increasing pride from seeing himself as a Big Guy, and seeing himself develop the confidence and the skills to start taking his place in the broad scheme of things. As a result, my top three tasks for mums with boys in this stage would be the following.

1 *Build confidence and competence.* The way you build
   confidence and competence is first to have confidence in
   him, and then to let him discover his competence. If you
   believe in him, he'll have no choice but to follow. The way
   to build his inner confidence is not through pep-talks or
   rousing speeches, but by letting him do things, including
   letting him fail. We learn more from our bloody knees
   than we ever do from pats on the back. This doesn't mean
   you push him over, but it does mean that you let him take
   chances.

2 *Build your relationship, because it will be his base for all that
   follows.* Building your relationship with him is hugely
   important. The teenage years are coming, and they will
   bring their own challenges, so now is the time to be laying
   in wood for winter. By the end of the second stage of his
   life he needs to know that you are on his side, just as surely
   as he knows that his bones will be there for his muscles to
   push against. He doesn't have to always like you, and he
   doesn't need to be your friend, but he does need to know
   that you are always there.

3 *Help him to connect action with consequence.* Helping him to
   connect action with consequence is also a biggie during this
   phase. He needs to begin to understand the complexities
   of action and consequence, because increasingly he will be
   making decisions that have far-ranging consequences. At
   six the biggest decision he might make is whether or not
   to take his coat to school, but by 11 he might be deciding
   whether to run the lights on his bike or whether he should
   stop. The more he understands the basic principle that
   everything he does has consequences, the better equipped
   he will be to make some of those bigger decisions.

My take on this stage of boy-ology is that it's an amazingly important time to finish off the groundwork you've been chipping away at so that he's ready for Stage Three, which obviously we'll get to in a minute. What this means is that you want to give him plenty of practice at making good decisions and thinking things through before he hits his teenage years. He's still a boy, but as he grows he's moving steadily closer to a key transition point, and so he's going to need plenty of time to make mistakes and to learn from them.

Here's my list of some must-do things for your Big Guys.

◇ Own and use a pocket knife without adult supervision.

◇ Build bigger huts in more distant places.

◇ Climb much taller trees.

◇ Acquire the skills not to fall out of the much taller trees.

◇ As he gets older (usually sometime around 8+ years), he should roam the streets with his friends without you being there.

◇ Walk to school (again usually sometime around 8+ years), by himself if possible, but a group will do. Either way, you shouldn't be there.

◇ Turn in an assignment late at school and get in trouble for it.

◇ Leave his coat at home and get cold and/or wet.

◇ Do this several more times until he gets the message.

◇ Make and fly a kite.

◇ Stay away from home for the night without you. Obviously, a friend's or grandparents' place is probably more preferable than a cardboard box under a bridge.

◇ Build a model plane, car or ship.

◇ Make a spear from a sharpened stick (which is why he needs the pocket knife) and throw it.

◇ Fire a bow and arrow.

◇ Build and light a fire.

◇ Learn to swim.

◇ Learn that when you're at the beach, you never take your eyes off the waves.

◇ Lose something precious.

◇ Go for a long walk in a wild and isolated place with you.

◇ Pizza and DVDs.

◇ Talk about anything and everything you can think of.

◇ Learn that Mum isn't your friend, she's your mum.

Big Guys bring with them a new and wondrous kind of fun. It's a slightly more hands-off kind of fun, because he needs to start to roam a little, but it's still incredible. This is where he practises being his own man, albeit a fledgling man, but a man just the same. Mistakes are important, and he needs to make as many as he can now so that he's learnt the lesson by the time he gets to the next bit. He also needs lots of hugs and cuddles, and all that lovely stuff. He'll probably ask for it less and less, but that doesn't mean he needs it any less.

Stage Three: Young Men
(12–19 years)
The bit where his part of the story begins

This is where it all starts to come together, and paradoxically where it all starts to fall apart a bit as well. The teenage years are when he begins to really come to grips with who and what he is. This is where he starts to make real choices that will influence the course of his life, but also where all boys go at least a little doolally.

Why doolally?

Essentially because there is an awful lot of development going on during adolescence, not just in their bodies, but in their brains as well. We're all pretty familiar with the whole puberty thing, but what a lot of people don't know is that there's an awful lot of brain development that goes on during adolescence in addition to all the pimples and loud music. I've written a lot about this in *Before Your Teenagers Drive You Crazy, Read This!*, but for our purposes here just let me sum it up by saying that teenagers aren't right in the head. They might look more and more like fully fledged people, but they aren't. In fact, it seems that we don't have a fully developed 'adult brain' until our mid-20s. This is why teenagers often seem moody, impulsive and reckless. It isn't just an attitude; it's their developing brains going through a phase of fairly intensive remodelling.

Part of this is that you need to have reasonable expectations of him during this period. Just because he looks like a sensible person doesn't mean he's always going to behave like one. Sometimes he may behave in ways that seem so staggeringly unreasonable, it will cause you to re-think the whole notion of having children. Sadly, by then it is far too late.

This is also a difficult time for mums because boys tend to become a little monosyllabic during this time. Where once there was a happy, cuddly little boy, now there is a tall, gangly, slightly stinky, ever-so-slightly moody, lumbering creature whose only mode of communication is to roll his eyes, shrug and say, 'I dunno'. Have no fear about any of this: this is just the way of Young Men. I'll talk more about communication with Young Men later on in Chapter 15. So far as tasks go, the following would be my top three recommendations.

1 *Don't freak out.* The trick here is not to give in to the fear. He's likely to do any one of a number of things that would alarm any sane person, but you need to keep hold of the fact that this is simply part of the ride. This is what Young Men do. There is a responsible, reasonable, rational adult in there, it's

just that it's going to be a little while before you see that part of him.

2 *Give him space, but not a vacuum.* Teenage boys need their space, but at the same time they also need boundaries and rules. The worst thing you can do is leave him to it, because he's not right in the head. By the same token, if you crowd him with too many rules and restrictions, you'll force him to rebel against them. Instead, you need to be constantly working on the balance between giving him room to do his thing and providing enough structure so you can contain some of the less sensible things he might be prone to doing.

3 *Hold the line.* Your most important job at this point is to make sure that once you've defined the limits, you hold fast to them. You're going to have to keep re-negotiating the limits as he grows, because he's going to need to wander farther and farther from home, but you need to stick to the rules that you've negotiated.

My list of must-do things for teenage boys is a little different than the previous two lists, because increasingly they're going to be making their own decisions about how they spend their spare time. Instead, it's more a list of things you should try to do with them over this time.

◊ Teach him to drive.

◊ Talk to him about girls (or boys).

◊ Model responsible behaviour with alcohol and drugs.

◊ Give him cuddles whenever you can get away with it.

◊ Tell him you love him, even if he rolls his eyes so far he runs the risk of spending the rest of his life looking at his own arse.

◊ Have at least one completely painful family holiday.

◊ Don't take any shit from him — that's not your job.

◊ Show him that women won't accept anything other than being treated with a basic level of respect.

◊ Always be there at his sports things, and his school things, even if he acts like he doesn't want you there. He may not, but later on he'll remember that you were there.

◊ Eat pizza and watch DVDs from time to time. It goes without saying that these should not be chick flicks, unless this is what he likes.

◊ Fart audibly from time to time . . . It'll surprise the hell out of him and let him know that you are unpredictable and mysterious.

Basically, surviving teenage boys isn't as hard as you might first imagine. The nice thing about time is that it does pass, and as it passes it drags even the most difficult boy closer and closer to being an adult. Even if he's a terrible adult, at least he's going to be able to get his own place.

2

What mums want

'So what do you want?' I asked Sally.

Her husband, Geoff, was seated beside her and had adopted the pose I'd long come to recognise as saying, 'Look, I really don't think we need to be here, so I'm just going to let her do all the talking.' Some people might see that as abrogating responsibility for parenting; others – most notably other fathers – might see it as simple pragmatism.

Either way, that seemed to be his position.

Sally looked at Geoff, briefly, and then started to speak: 'I want to know how to get him to pick up his clothes, and keep his room clean, and I want to be able to ask him to do something without him sulking or glaring at me.'

The 'him' in this case was Josh, their 13-year-old son. He was the older of two, having been blessed with an annoying little sister two years his junior. They loved each other about as much as North Korea loves South Korea.

'OK,' I said. 'Anything else?'

'Lots,' said Sally. 'I'd also like to be able to actually have a conversation with him that includes more than three words, and I'd like to know what's going on in his life.'

'And?'

'And I'd like for him to take more interest in his studies, and to get a little more focused on school. Whenever I bring it up, he acts like I'm Attila the Hun.'

'Attila the Hun?'

She nodded. 'I can't say anything without him going off at me and yelling at me for nagging.'

'What else?' I was sure the list wasn't done yet.

'I'd just like some small sign that he's growing up to be a responsible young man and not some grungy, surly deadbeat who just wants to lie on his bed and play computer games all day.'

'Anything else before we kick off?'

'I'd like to be able to give him a cuddle every now and again without him acting like it makes him sick.'

I smiled. 'OK,' I said.

'"OK" – you can do all that?' she asked.

'Nope.'

She frowned. 'How much of it can you do?'

I scrunched up my face in an act of exaggerated calculation.

'I'd say . . . probably . . . almost none of it.'

'Almost none of it?'

'Yep.'

'Oh.'

I shrugged fatalistically, which is not an easy thing to do while seated.

'Well . . . ?' She seemed a little lost for words.

'Look, you wouldn't want me to do that anyway.'

'I *would*.'

'No, you wouldn't. The only way for me to do all that would be to saw off the top of his head, scoop all the goopy stuff out and replace it with an iPod.'

Geoff laughed. Sally looked a little hurt.

'The truth is that most parents have a shopping list of stuff that they'd like their kids to be like. Me, I'd like for my boys to have a burning interest in the military so that they could one day join the SAS and I could finally get the chance to fire a heavy machine gun – but I've had to accept that that isn't going to happen.'

'I don't want machine guns,' Sally said. 'I just want him to be more . . . I don't know . . . more . . .'

'More like you'd want him to be?'

'No . . . well . . . yes, a little maybe.'

'See, now that's the part I can't do. I can't make him be what he isn't, but I can help you to understand him a little more, and I can tell you about some of the tricks when it comes to raising boys. I can't change him, but I can help you to understand a bit more about how he ticks, and how you can make life a little easier between you and him. Will that do?'

She thought for a moment, then nodded.

'Good,' I said. 'Now, let's first get clear about the difference between what you *want* and what you can actually *do*.'

'So what's the difference?' she asked.

'Well, let's take Geoff here,' I said. 'See, he *wants* to be back at work because he thinks that's much more important than this, but he's about to *do* something quite different and have a conversation with me about what Josh needs. Right, Geoff?'

Geoff swallowed and sat up slightly straighter in his chair. 'Uh, yeah. Of course.'

Spread the love is my policy.

I think it would be fair to say that most mums are, to varying degrees, a lot like Sally in that they don't want much. They simply have the very reasonable wish that everything be perfect. They want their children to be healthy, and happy, and clean. Clean is actually very important to most mums. Dads might uncharitably think that mums might be a little *too* concerned with kids being clean, but then mums might rightly reply that dads are sometimes a little too negligent on that front.

Mums also want their children to look nice, which is difficult if dad dresses the children, because he will sometimes choose clothes that clash ridiculously. Mums are irritated by holes in the knees of trousers, and it grates them terribly that boys seem to have an almost preternatural ability to wear holes in the knees of said trousers within seconds of putting them on. Mums find it difficult to understand how holes can appear so quickly when boys seem to spend all their time running around.

Nutritionally, mothers have high expectations. They want boys to eat lots of fruit and vegetables, which is entirely reasonable, and indeed laudable. Mothers tend to provide breakfasts for young children that are beyond reproach. Said breakfasts will usually contain a good mix of minerals, vitamins, whole grains and fresh produce. Contrast this with a typical dad breakfast, which is usually anything wrapped in plastic that they can grab from the cupboard: muesli bars, raisins, candles, anything.

Mums want their boys to do well in school. They want their boys to do their homework gladly, and to put their all into whatever task they're set. Because mums know how much their boys are capable of, they want their boys to achieve at the level they're capable of. Mums want their boys to develop a good work ethic, and to come to see the value of having things organised and completed ahead of time.

Socially, mums want their boys to be friends with the nice boys. They do not want their boys to be friends with the bad boys. Mums particularly like their boys to buddy up with well-mannered, clean, well brought-up boys. Mums like the kind of boys who say 'please' and 'thank you', and who are nice to their own mums.

Mums don't necessarily want their boys to have girlfriends, but they understand that there isn't much they can do to stop it. As a result, they want their boys to meet and form relationships with nice girls from nice families. They generally do not like tattoos or piercings. They very reasonably want their boys to treat their girlfriends with respect and courtesy.

Mums also want their boys to get good jobs. They want their sons to have fulfilling careers, doing the kinds of things that would make them proud. They want their boys to become decent men, upstanding members of the community who contribute and make a positive difference.

Finally, they want their sons to marry nice girls and provide lots of grandchildren. A granddaughter would be nice. They sometimes daydream about how lovely it would be to have a little girl to take shopping and buy all the pink girly nonsense they never got to buy for their own kids.

All this is very reasonable, and very normal. In fact, I want all that stuff for my own boys – possibly with the exception of the healthy breakfasts, which I have to admit I'm a little slack about. And I'm not even a mum. I'd venture to suggest that all that stuff is what we all want for our kids, both mums and dads.

Sadly, though, it's just about completely impossible. The only parents whose children achieve this degree of actual perfection are people who later discover that their children are in fact tightly buttoned serial killers.

For the rest of us, our kids' lives are a little messier.

3

A curious paradox

Paradox (*noun*) a statement or situation that contains two opposite facts or characteristics, making it seem impossible or difficult to understand

The curious thing about some mums is that despite the fact that they really want to know more about what makes their sons tick, and how to communicate with them more effectively, they don't always want to change how they are with their boys. They'll listen politely, and then proceed to tell you how what you're saying doesn't apply to them because they don't do that. Which is the curious paradox: knowing that what you're doing isn't working terribly well, but at the same time resisting the suggestion that some change is necessary to get things going again.

Let me show you what I mean.

Julie came to see me because she was having bitter arguments with her 10-year-old son, Matthew. None of it was over big stuff, it was all the usual humdrum details that are the meat and potatoes of family life: socks left lying about, plates not put in the sink, clothes lost at school, grumpiness at shower time. The content of their conflict might have been all very normal, but it was the process of how they went about arguing that was the real problem.

'Tell him,' Julie said to Matthew.

The boy just shrugged his shoulders in an angry, disconnected kind of way as he slumped on one end of the couch.

'Go on,' Julie repeated. 'Tell him.'

Now, I wouldn't want you to get the impression at this point that the problem is that Julie's just bossy. Actually, she is a very likeable person. I liked her the moment she walked in and sat down. No particular reason, some people you just do.

'Maybe you could kick things off?' I suggested to her.

'He doesn't show me any kind of respect anymore,' she said.

'How do you mean?' Not the most amazing and insightful of questions, I know, but it usually does the job.

'Any time I ask him to do anything, he just grunts, or complains or is rude to me.'

I looked at Matthew, who was in turn glaring at the arm of the chair as if it were just about to make some smartass comment. He looked a nice enough boy, but I could see that he had a bit of a grumpy lean to him.

'You think that's fair?' I asked him.

He shrugged, which, all things considered, was not an unreasonable response.

'Well?' Julie asked him. 'Am I being unfair?'

He shrugged, and muttered, 'I dunno.'

'You don't know? How can you not know? Either I'm being fair or I'm being unfair. What is there not to know?'

Matthew shrugged again, perhaps hoping that the old saying was wrong and that it was in fact 'a shrug in time saves nine'. 'Fair, I guess . . .'

He looked like he was struggling with something, but then Julie broke in: 'How can you possibly say that when you keep blowing up every time I say anything about anything?' She waited for a moment to see if he'd respond – at least two seconds. 'I don't think I ask anything of you that's unreasonable, do I? Do I? Well?'

Each question mark was followed by an ample second-and-a-half gap for him to answer if he wanted to.

Matthew didn't avail himself of these microburst invitations to chat, and instead abandoned shrugging completely, opting for the full-bodied slump instead.

Seeing where this was all headed, I stepped in and asked Matthew to step out of the room for a bit while I talked about him with his mum.

No point lying about that one.

'Julie,' I said, 'there are two things we can do here. The first is that I can be dreadfully polite and dance around the edges of what I think is going on here because I don't want to risk offending you.'

She looked at me. 'And the second?'

'Well, the second is that I could just be incredibly direct without worrying too much about offending you and tell you exactly what I think.'

'Let's do that,' she said. 'I'd rather know what you think.'

'It could be rough,' I said.

'I'm a big girl.'

'You sure?'

'Yep.'

I nodded. 'OK.'

'So what do you think, then?'

'Do you ever shut up and let the boy speak?'

She looked at me for a moment, and for a brief, pulse-elevating moment I thought I might have misjudged her, then she burst out laughing.

Phew.

'Seriously, though,' I said once she'd stopped. 'You're a good mum, I get that, and you love him heaps, I get that, too. He knows it as well, and he loves you, too. I get all that. But you don't give him much room to say anything, or even to think about what you've said.'

'I do,' she said. 'He just doesn't answer me. What am I supposed to do if he won't speak?'

'Stop talking?' I said, in that tone you use when you're half-asking, half-suggesting.

'If I did that, no one would say anything,' she said.

'Well, that's one possibility,' I said. 'But the other possibility is that if you stop saying quite so much, he might say a little more.'

'I doubt it,' she said. 'If I didn't say anything, we'd live in a completely silent house.'

This time I shrugged. 'I don't think so. Actually I think the real problem here is that you're caught in a fairly typical vicious cycle.'

'Which is?'

'You talk too much, he shuts down, so you talk more, so he shuts down more, and so on and so on.'

'I don't talk too much,' she said. 'I actually make a real effort to ask him questions.'

I nodded. 'You do, that's true, but you don't give him much time to respond.'

She frowned, 'How long does he *need*?'

I shrugged again: 'Anything from a minute to two days.'

She looked to see if I was joking.

I wasn't.

'That's ridiculous,' she said.

'I know, but there you go.'

'Well, I think the real issue is that he needs to learn to be more open about his feelings. He needs to learn to express himself more politely.'

'That I'd agree with, at least the polite bit anyway,' I said, 'but I think you need to re-adjust your expectations around speed of delivery and word limit.'

'I'm sure I probably can slow down a bit, but he needs to learn how to express more clearly what's going on.'

We were on opposite sides at this moment, and nothing

good ever comes from those kind of 'I'm right, you're wrong' arguments.

Time for a change of direction.

'Can I ask a more personal question?' I said.

'Yes.'

'Does he ever leave drips of wee on the toilet floor?'

She laughed again. 'Constantly. Drives me nuts.'

'Do you know why that is?' I asked.

She shook her head. 'Apart from the obvious issue of lack of attention and being a piglet, no.'

'Let me explain . . .'

Now, we'll get to that vexing issue of the wee drips ourselves later on, but just for now let's focus on the curious paradox of why when mums know they have a problem, they're often reluctant to listen to advice that entails any kind of real change.

The thing is that it isn't just mums, though; it's me, too. Actually, it's you as well. Truth be told, it's *all* of us. You see, despite the fact that we all like to think we're objective, rational, conscious thinkers, it turns out we're not. We naïvely assume our brains are simply squishy grey computers that we use with clear and conscious intent, but the truth is a little more surprising. There is now very good evidence that, far from being objective computers, our brains are actually pulling all kinds of strings.

In a very amusing, very well researched and very surprising book, Australian cognitive neuroscientist Dr Cordelia Fine convincingly demonstrates that our brains are in fact simultaneously vain, emotional, immoral, deluded, pig-headed, secretive, weak-willed and bigoted. It turns out that our brains, quite literally, have a mind of their own.

We like to think that we see the world as it is and make decisions 'based on the facts', but our brains actually do quite a lot to protect us from the harsher realities of the world. We are much better equipped at finding fault in others, and not so well designed to find it in ourselves. How often, just as a for instance, do you discuss with your other half, or a close friend, or the little you who lives inside your head, the shortcomings of other parents? I'd wager that if I asked you to list off the parenting shortcomings of your extended family, friends, associates, neighbours or even complete strangers you happen to observe in a café, you would find this easier than listing off your own faults.

Our brains seem to be automatically programmed to protect our fragile egos by actively 'sieving' the facts and pulling all kinds of tricks to ensure that we always see ourselves in the best light possible. This doesn't mean that we're simply egotistical blowhards who puff out our feathers at every opportunity; instead, according to the very coolly named Dr Cordelia Fine, the process is much more subtle. For example, we tend to remember the more positive things about our character and we forget the bits that aren't so palatable. And when we actually do something bad, our brains actively look for extenuating circumstances: the 'Yes, I did it, but it wasn't so bad because . . .' defence.

The very reason I use a lot of case studies in my books is that it's far easier for us to see others' errors than our own. If I make the case studies about you, then I'm immediately pitted against a raft of inbuilt psychological mechanisms that protect you from seeing the things you might be doing yourself.

I'm no different. I spend my days giving people sage and wise advice about how to raise their children, and then go home and make many of the same mistakes myself. I can be preaching patience and understanding at 3.00pm and then be engaged in a full-fledged rant only a few hours later.

And, if asked, I'd probably give you some monkey shite about how what I was doing wasn't really bad because of this reason, or was actually helpful because of that reason. Indeed, this is the very reason that when I'm having problems with my own boys I pretend that my family is a client I'm working with, because that's the only way I've found to get my own vain brain out of the way. I have to fake my brain out by pretending it isn't me, then applying the results once I've figured out a plan for 'them'.

What's more, we tend to be completely befuddled by our emotions. The more worked up we get by something, the less likely we are to approach it rationally. We are also – and by this I mean the universal 'we' – stubborn to the core. The stubborn nature of our brains is particularly relevant to what we're talking about here. You are very likely to nod in agreement and appreciation of my sage wisdom when I say things you agree with, and then find all kinds of reasons to discount what I'm saying if I say things with which you disagree. You might, as the more obvious example, conclude something along the lines of 'Well, a man would say something like that, wouldn't he?'

Time and time again the research has shown that we are very good at finding reasons why the people who think the same as we do are more onto it, and equally we are good at reasoning why the people who disagree with us are halfwits.

Like I said, it isn't just you: it's me as well. This has absolutely nothing to do with gender, because we *all* do this stuff. My reason for bringing all this up, though, is to gently suggest that you bear all this in mind when you're reading what follows. Keep an open mind is all I'm saying, and just remember that your brain will be sitting on your shoulder looking for any way it can to filter out any less-comfortable truths.

And speaking of uncomfortable truths, it's time for a few of my own.

My glass house and a handful of stones

It seems only fair, given that I'm going to be spending the next couple of hundred pages telling mums how to do their job, that I begin with a little honesty about my own inadequacies as a parent. Obviously I'd look far better if I just told a bunch of lies about my own parenting skills, but that wouldn't be right. I think it's far more helpful if all our shortcomings are out there on the table at the start. The other reason I think it's so important to declare one's inadequacies upfront is that it will allow you to put everything that I'm about to say in some kind of context. Context is important – very important – because the context always shapes the message.

I always tell the families I see that they should be wary about anyone giving you parenting advice, even me. Especially me. I think you should know some things about where that advice is coming from. We're all used-car salesmen in this business, so you should know what our interest is in whatever idea or opinion we're trying to sell you.

For my part, it's no small irony that I'm now spending increasingly more of my time writing parenting books. The irony comes from the fact that I think parenting books are actually a large part of the problem. We've all become so afraid of doing the wrong thing that sometimes it feels a little like they need to run special postgraduate courses at university to teach us how to raise our kids.

And despite all this well-meaning advice, it seems to me that parents are actually becoming *less* confident, not more confident. If knowledge is power, then how come I'm seeing so many parents who feel varying degrees of powerlessness?

It has long been my view that we're the most informed generation of parents ever. We have to contend with things that our parents never knew about. They didn't know about ADHD, or self-esteem, or the Mozart Effect, so they simply got on with the business of raising kids unburdened with all the worry. Mums are particularly vulnerable to worry, and we'll talk more about why that is in a little while, but just for now let me say that I think mums have been fed a fairly consistent diet of anxiety-producing information for far too long. Information can sometimes be empowering, and sometimes it can just do your head in.

So my answer to the problem of too many books is to write yet another book?

Yup, pretty much.

(Insert uncomfortable silence here.)

So what kind of a parent am I?

Well, before we get into that, let me tell you what kind of son I am. My dad was a good guy, a builder, musician and lover of sports. He was married to my mother for 43 years, and over that time they raised four of us: my older brother, me, a younger brother and my baby sister. My dad was a good bloke who was involved in my life in the way that good dads of that era were. I don't recall us ever building a Lego tower together at six in the morning as modern dads do, but I never doubted for one second that he was on my side.

Not one second.

The only unresolved father issues I have are that I wish he was still here. My father died in 2003, and there isn't a day goes by when I don't wish he'd had a little more time to be grandad to my two sons.

My mother is the kind of mum I wish more people in the world had, because if they did it would be a much nicer world to live in. She never worked outside the home, although that wasn't so much about politics as it was about the fact there weren't really many jobs around that fitted in with raising four kids back then. We didn't have a lot of money, and I'm sure a second wage would have made their lives a little less stressful back then. My mum drove me the normal amount of crazy when I was a kid, because she'd fuss and worry, but that was long before I understood that this is simply what good mums do. She still worries, and probably always will. She often tells me I look tired, or I'm too busy, or that I eat too fast.

She always will worry, because that is the fate of good mothers everywhere.

My only unresolved mother issue is that I wish she'd lay off telling me not to eat so fast. Aside from that, she's great. Actually, it's taken me quite a while to work out that it's precisely *because* of the fact she still worries about me eating too fast that she is so great.

OK, then, so what kind of parent am I?

Well, I've got two boys, currently aged six and nine. I love them more than I ever knew it was possible to love another human being, and yet despite that they still frequently make me feel like running as far as my legs will carry me to some quieter, sunnier place where I could start again in a new, peaceful, childless life.

It's funny, isn't it? Those we love the most can also make us feel like fleeing for our very lives.

I like talking about monkeys with my boys. I'm not sure why, I just do. I particularly delight in telling my older son stories about Matumba the Monkey King (pronounced Ma-*tuhmmm*-ba). He hates these stories with a passion. They drive him crazy, which, for reasons I am unable to explain, just makes me want to tell them more.

I have almost uncontrollable urges to lie to my youngest son whenever he asks me anything.

'Dadda?' he might ask me.

'What, son?'

'Where's Mama?' he might reasonably ask, having noticed that his mother is no longer in the room.

'She's run off to be a pirate,' I tell him. 'She's poked out an eye, swapped her hand for a hook and glued a parrot on her shoulder. She's promised to bring us back some treasure, though, which is good news for you and me, because we can take it all to McDonald's and eat cheeseburgers 'til we're as fat as a couple of fat old monkeys.'

Fortunately for him, he's finally realised that I'm a dreadful liar and has learnt to simply ask again until he gets a sensible answer.

One day I suspect that all this lying will end tragically.

'Run, son!' I will yell frantically. 'Lions! Run away!'

And he will look at me and smirk. 'Yeah, right.'

Now, the lying and the monkeys aside, let me give you some specific examples of what a rubbish job I do from time to time.

When my eldest son was 18 months old, we were out walking one day. He was in one of those backpack things, and when we got back to the car I took off the pack and set it down on the ground on its metal frame while I unlocked the car. Unfortunately we were on a hill, and that combined with his big-headed centre of gravity meant that when my back was turned, he toppled forward and face-planted into the concrete footpath. Oops.

Funnily enough, I did the exact same thing with my younger son when he was about the same age. Oops again.

I once knowingly and wilfully let my three-year-old son crash his bike into a bamboo bush. He wasn't concentrating on braking techniques, and I thought if he crashed it would improve the whole actions (or rather lack of actions) have consequences learning-from-experience routine. Sadly, a bamboo shoot had broken off just at three-year-old eye-height, which he duly connected with. There were tears, and blood, but his eyes were fine. For my part, I got a bit of a telling-off from his mum.

I have yelled at my precious boys.

They have made me so angry that once I had to go have a lie-down because my head hurt. Actually I thought I was about to have a stroke, which was provoked by the pounding, throbbing sensation of pain deep in my brain.

I've lost them from time to time when we've been out places as well. Easy to do, really, when they're below eye-level and you have to keep looking down all the time.

I also have a dangerous tendency to get so wrapped up in what's going on in my world that I sometimes forget that my most important job is them. Just the night before last when my older son asked me if we could have a chat when he was lying in bed, I brushed him off because I had this book to write. I told him, 'Not tonight, another night'.

Later, when I went in to kiss him goodnight, he was reading and I asked him whether he was enjoying the book. He pointed out, correctly, that if I was really interested I would have stayed for a talk in the first place.

Those are the moments you get pulled up so hard you feel your chest ache.

Last night we talked for half an hour before bed, and it made us both feel far better than a thousand or so more words in this manuscript could ever do. I care about this book, don't get me wrong, but I care about him more. Unless of course this thing becomes a *New York Times* bestseller, in which case I'd obviously need to re-evaluate the whole 'who do I love more' thing.

I could go on, but I'm sure you get the point. None of us is perfect, and I'm no exception. I have done many, many stupid things with my boys, but like all kids they seem to have cottoned on to the fact that not everything always goes to plan. They have to survive me raising them just as I have to try to survive them. We all have to try to get out with as much of our sanity and health intact as we can.

All parents – you, me, all of us – have our less-than-shining moments.

So, if in the pages that follow you start feeling a little annoyed, or maybe unfairly judged, then at least you can comfort yourself with the fact that you haven't dropped all your children on their heads like I have.

Unless of course you've done this as well, in which case you're every bit as rubbish as I am.

Two

The Great Big Boy Debate

If you've got a boy, then you may have heard that the sky is falling. Or you may have heard that instead of falling, the sky's actually clearing and the sun is coming out. There seem to be wildly differing accounts of the state of the boy nation, and it can be hard to know which way you should jump.

In this section we're going to focus on the debate, on the claims and the counterclaims.

We're going to look at the statistics to see what that stuff really means and how it applies to your boy(s).

We're also going to look at what some of the latest and greatest neuroscience can tell us about our kids. There are all kinds of claims being made about this stuff by all kinds of people, so I think it's important we all understand enough about it to be able to figure out how much weight we should give it.

Next, we'll go on an imaginary field trip to Wisconsin to tackle international terrorism, take on street crime and learn some pretty amazing things about just how different boys and girls really are.

Finally, we'll spend some time looking at the place where the boy debate really starts to smoke: the classroom. How are boys really doing in school? Have our schools become hostile towards boy culture? Are they failing? Are single-sex schools the answer?

All that and an interesting story about infanticidal beetles.

Oh, and the good news here is that, at least in my humble opinion, there actually is good news here.

5

Is the sky really falling?

First we raise the dust, then claim we cannot see.

Charles Berkeley

Chicken Little was clearly a bit of a drama queen. As we all know, the popular Aesop's fable describes how Chicken Little gets hit on the head with an acorn one day and then completely freaks out. Not just that he gets slightly concerned, or a little perturbed, but completely and utterly freaked out. Rather than trying to figure out what the hell just happened, Chicken Little decides on the basis of that one bump that the sky is falling. This understandably causes the chicken some distress, and obviously immediately necessitates a trip to the King to warn him of the impending end of all things.

Along the way, Chicken Little is joined by a number of other oddly named friends (for example, Henny Penny, Cocky Locky and the indomitable Goosey Loosey) of similarly nervous disposition, who join in the crusade. At some point they meet up with the stupidly named, but craftily inclined, Foxy Loxy, who hatches and – depending on which version of the story you read – cleverly executes an evil plan to eat them all.

The moral of the story is that you should not believe everything you're told (or read), and this seems a timely fable to begin this chapter.

Actually, you've already made one mistake in that regard and we haven't even got started. It turns out that 'Chicken Little' isn't one of Aesop's fables, and further that Chicken Little isn't even a chicken. In fact, the story originates from Indian Buddhist folklore, and in particular a collection of stories called *The Jataka Tales*, where the chicken is actually a hare, and the acorn is a mango. Also, there's no fox but instead a wise lion, who's a previous incarnation of the Buddha and who guides the hare back to the mango tree and points out the mistake, thus calming everybody down.

So I told you something that wasn't true, and you bought it. You see how that happened? I said, 'As we all know, the popular Aesop's fable describes how Chicken Little gets hit on the head . . .' and you just sailed right past it, believing me. It really is as simple as that, because not many of us actually bother to check the facts of what we read or what people tell us. This makes it very easy to say just about any old thing and get away with it.

The slightly more refined moral of the Jataka tale of 'The Hare and the Mango' is that you should use your own reasoning and experience to decide what a given something means rather than simply believing what other people tell you. In fact, Buddha himself said – and I'm paraphrasing here a bit – don't believe something to be true just because you read it, or see it on the evening news, or some Discovery Channel documentary, or because some teacher or preacher tells you it's true; believe something to be true only when you have tested it and evaluated it for yourself.

Good advice, and something parents would be wise to remember.

So in that light, let's take a look at what they're saying about boys and how they're doing, and then, perhaps even more importantly, let's take a look at what the numbers really say.

'Boys are three times more likely to die by age 21 than girls'

Holy crap.

Sounds pretty dire, don't you think?

Actually, by a strange quirk of coincidence this statement was made by a parenting 'expert' on television as I was in the process of researching this very chapter. As the father of two boys, and even knowing all that I know about this stuff, it still made a little reflex shiver run up my spine.

Then I caught myself and got my feet back on the ground.

'How can people say that stuff?' I asked my wife.

'I know,' she said.

'It serves no useful purpose; it just scares people.'

'I know.'

'Saying stuff like "three times more likely to die" is completely bloody meaningless.'

'I know.'

'I mean, what the hell relevance is that statistic to anyone raising a boy in the real world?'

'I know,' she said again. By now she's gotten used to my occasional indignant outbursts at the television and has learnt just to nod in agreement until my muted outrage has passed.

So why was this such a meaningless statement?

Well, it's meaningless because it is talking about general level averages when really what matters for you is your individual boy. That statement does not mean that *all* boys are three times more likely to die by age 21, because, quite simply, they aren't. What I think he meant — and I'm just guessing here, because this hugely alarming statement wasn't put in any sort of context — is that he'd done some kind of calculation and added up the proportion of boys who die from all kinds of different causes and compared that to the number of girls who died from similar causes, and ended up with a number that was larger for boys than girls.

What you have to do, though, is stop for a moment and *really* try to focus on what that number *means* in any practical sense. I would suggest that at the individual level, at the level of you and your boy, it is a largely meaningless statistic.

Let's stop for a moment and look at the major causes of death for boys and young men. Obviously this is not very happy material, so I'm not going to dwell on it for long. Still there's a point here that needs to be made, so I'll make it as quickly as I can and we'll move on to happier things.

For children, the major causes of death are illness and injury. So far as illness goes in children, there isn't much you can do about that other than the basics, which is immunisation and trying to live a healthy life. The accidents part we can do something about, but sometimes accidents happen despite all the precautions in the world.

In young men, the two leading causes of death most places in the world are suicide and car accidents. We'll talk about cars some more in Chapter 20, but it should come as no surprise that boys are more likely to die in car accidents than girls, because boy culture is inherently more risk-taking than girl culture. Boys tend to do more risky things than girls. Always have, and probably always will. We'll see later in Chapter 14 that this risk-taking aspect of boys' nature is a feature observed in boys of all ages right throughout the world. We'll probably never change the fact that boys are more likely to do dangerous stuff than girls are.

The other leading cause of death in young men is suicide. In the UK for every 1 girl who dies by suicide there are 3.3 boys who die. This is clearly a troubling statistic. From the 1990s onwards, suicide rates actually began to steadily decline; in 2005 they were at their lowest for 30 years. Then in 2007–2008 the rate started to climb, rising by 8% among men and 9% among women.

And the reason for this rise?

In 2008 a bunch of greedy bankers on Wall Street dropped the imaginary financial balls they'd been juggling and plunged the rest of us into a global financial crisis we're still dealing with today. During the Great Depression suicide rates soared and recent research in the UK has found that for every 10% rise in unemployment, there is a 1.4% rise in suicide. Hard times are sometimes too hard for some people to bear.

So after decades of shrinking risk in the UK and a number of other countries, the figures have climbed back the other way. Alarming? Yes, but here's the thing: whether the official statistics for suicide risk (or shark attack risk, or meteor strike risk, or even spontaneous human combustion risk for that matter) are rising, or falling, or staying the same, that isn't what *really* matters. What *really* matters to everyday mums is not how *all* boys are doing, but how *your boy* is doing. Be especially wary of anyone who uses scare tactics to get your attention. Statistics can be helpful, but they can all too often make you so worried you can lose sight of the important stuff.

The boy brain:
fact or fad?

Shoe stores have always seemed to me to be incontrovertible proof that males and females are simply made of different stuff. My wife loves them, not in an Imelda Marcos, morally corrupt kind of way, but she certainly likes them a lot. If we're passing a shoe store and she has time, she'll pop in for a browse. For reasons I cannot fathom, just the act of looking at shoes is reward enough; she doesn't actually have to buy them to enjoy the experience.

I, on the other hand, think shoe stores are the psychological equivalent of necrotising fasciitis, the flesh-eating bacteria that does just what its name implies: it eats you alive, cell by cell. This might seem a little extreme for many of the mums reading this, but I don't think you know how dull most men find shoe stores. You see, when most men look at shoes we evaluate them not only by how they look, but also by how we think they might function if we were running away from something – a crazed gunman, for instance – or if the tread is sufficient to scale a cliff in an as-yet-unforseen emergency. I myself have never had to scale a cliff in an emergency, but I have passed up several pairs of shoes that did not look up to the task on the off-chance that that situation might arise.

Nice shoes, I have thought, *but they've got no tread on them. I couldn't climb a rock face in those.*

I know, it's crazy, but many of us blokes judge the suitability of a pair of shoes not just by colour and style, but also by how fast we think we can run, climb and, yes, sometimes even swim in them. This latter point is important because if your plane crashes into the sea, then you want your shoes to stay on so you can both kick sharks and also hike through the jungle to get help once you've reached land. And it's a pretty safe bet that if you do hit land, then there's going to be a perilous cliff that will need to be scaled before you can reach the actual jungle.

By these measures, the majority of women's shoes are, quite simply, ridiculous. With the high heels and the tiny little straps, it seems a miracle to us that you can even walk in them. We don't understand why anyone would want to strap their feet into devices that seem expressly designed to make any kind of running, climbing or jumping over charging lions completely impossible. Those are the kind of shoes that get you killed.

And yet still my wife picks up a pair of shoes that look like something the Spanish Inquisition had dreamt up and asks me what I think.

What do I think?

I think that men and women are so different in so many ways that it must be hardwired. There have to be stark differences between the way that men's and women's brains are wired together, because that's the only thing that can explain women's shoe stores. Forget Mars and Venus, I'm thinking it's like some whole other dimension.

And my guess is that for the majority of women, if I tried to explain – just as an example – why when men are standing on the balcony of an apartment or office block they will automatically work out in their heads how they could either climb up the building they're on from balcony to balcony, or they will try to calculate if they could jump across to the next building or rooftop . . . (We won't actually do it, mind you, but the Peter Pan part of every man that never really dies in most of us will always go through the drill.) For most women, I'm sure Mars and Venus would also seem a bit of an understatement at that point.

There is something about the idea of a male brain and a female brain that just seems, well, sensible. The notion certainly has a huge appeal, and the reading public consumes this stuff in staggering amounts.

But is all this talk of male and female brains on the level? What has science really shown us about the difference between the male brain and the female brain? And what are the implications for those of us raising boys?

All it takes is a sprinkle of neuroscience

There is no doubt that if you want to sexy things up when you're talking about kids, then a little neuroscience goes a long way. We all love neuroscience. The media loves neuroscience. Hell, you'd have to be some kind of miserable soul not to. It looks great, it sounds great, it's just plain great.

If you go to Google Image Search and type in 'fMRI', you can't help but be impressed at just how amazingly clever we human beings are. We'll get back to what fMRIs are all about later in the chapter, but just for now I'd suggest that if you look at the pictures that come up when you search that term you will be forced to admit that, while we might share 99% of our genetic material with chimpanzees, there must be something pretty damn good in that final 1% that makes a pretty damn big difference. They sit in trees and sniff each other's arses while we sit in fancy buildings looking at very pretty pictures of the inside of people's heads.

As a result of the complete coolness of neuroscience, there have been some pretty big stories (and books).

Perhaps the best place to start is by looking at a few of the commonly accepted differences between men and women that have been reported widely in the media (CNN, *The New York Times*, *Time magazine*, the BBC and the like) over the past couple of years. This is the stuff that you've probably stumbled across in one place or another over recent years:

◊ Girls' and boys' brains are 'hardwired' completely differently. They're so different in fact that it's almost like they're from different planets.

◊ On average, women talk quite a lot more than men. (A figure that continues to be widely reported in the media is that women speak on average 20,000 words a day, and men speak only 7,000.)

◊ Research shows that boys have a disconnection between the emotional centres of their brain and the communication centres of their brain. This is why boys find it hard to talk about their feelings.

◊ Research shows that newborn girls demonstrate a clear preference for looking at people's faces, whereas boys show a clear preference for looking at moving objects.

◊ Girls' and boys' eyes are hardwired differently, which is why girls use lots of colours in their drawings and boys tend to use only a few, darker colours.

◊ Girls' hearing is about seven times more sensitive than boys', so boys tend not to hear softly spoken female teachers.

◊ Depending on who you listen to, brain scans have shown that boys' brain development is anywhere from 6 months to 2.5 years behind girls when they start school.

When you read through that list it all seems fairly reasonable, and more than a little frightening. If you bounce around the internet a bit, you'll find all kinds of people repeating this stuff, including paediatricians, psychologists, teachers, parents and politicians. This stuff has quickly become the accepted line when it comes to the 'developing picture' of gender and the brain, and it's one of the central pillars of the people who are driving the 'boy crisis' message.

And it's just so darn compelling.

But of course, the obvious question has to be asked: how come we ended up with such vastly different blobby grey lumps in our heads?

Garnish with a little Darwin

Well, this is where a little shuck and jive with evolutionary theory and natural selection often comes in. One of the various rationales for these hardwired differences often quoted is that in the dim prehistoric times women and men had very different roles. Women gathered fruit, nuts, insects and roots, and so had more sensitive and nimble fingers. They also looked after the little cavebabies, and so they hardwired their brains accordingly with a more finely tuned social sense, and a tendency to be more aware of what was going on around them in the group. Women adapted to become the insect-gathering, baby-raising networkers.

Men, on the other hand, went off and killed large mammals. This required a certain amount of recklessness and self-sacrifice, and not a small amount of courage. We men didn't need to develop our ability to empathise and understand how other people were feeling, because we were too busy killing big hairy elephants and the like.

Sounds pretty reasonable, right?

Which is, of course, the problem. You start spinning some line about cavemums huddled around the fire raising cavebabies and picking up berries, and you straight away start thinking that it does sound pretty reasonable that they'd be spending a bit of time developing girl-talk as they went about their gathering. Just like it sounds reasonable that cavemen were too busy trying not to get squashed to worry about whether the caveguy next to them was feeling vulnerable, or perhaps underappreciated. But there's another take that leads to the completely opposite conclusion.

You see, one of the things about the early humans was that

they tended to live in small groups, and from time to time they'd come up against other small groups. Remember that this was long before lawyers had been invented, and so they had to figure out what to do for themselves when they encountered other groups. I think you could make a pretty good case for the fact that, if you're standing facing off from a bunch of strangers with spears and clubs and the like, you're going to need to develop some quite good skills at guessing how others are feeling. We have been social animals from the very beginning, and so to co-exist with other humans we needed to be able to read what they are feeling.

And who are the people you're going to shove out the front to try to understand how the opposing spear-carriers are feeling? Men, that's who. So rather than having no interest in judging how other people are feeling, I would think that men would need to develop quite good skills in this regard if they wanted to avoid a spear though their gizzards.

What's more, it seems a little silly to say that women just had to gather nuts and berries and raise babies. While they probably did have to do that, it's worth reflecting on the fact that they didn't just pop down to the local Palaeolithic supermarket to do it. It wasn't like *The Flintstones*. They had little things like 500-kilogram sabre-toothed tigers, giant wolves and eagles big enough to carry off people to worry about. They were gathering berries in the same places that ferocious carnivorous animals were also hunting and gathering *them*. Do you think it's just possible that being a cavemum required a little self-sacrifice and completely reckless bravery from time to time?

While these types of explanations might appeal to some of the rather well-worn stereotypes we have about men and women (even cavemen and cavewomen), I'm not sure they're particularly helpful. Unless of course you're trying to find some kind of evolutionary-based justification for differences in the hardwiring of male and female brains. Then it's bloody useful indeed.

Science is a great thing, and it has helped us to make staggering advances in all kinds of areas. That said, science – or, more accurately, opinion dressed up as 'science' – can also be an elaborate smokescreen to make a wacky idea sound like the kind of thing Albert Einstein himself would have approved of.

Read on and I'll show you how easy it is.

It turns out Dad's not lazy;
it's in his genes

It's a piece of cake to take a piece of science and turn it into a piece of politically driven poppycock. Let me give you an example of how easy it would be for me to spin you a clever little tale, based on a real piece of research, to justify why it's more natural for dads to leave all the hands-on parenting work to mothers.

On 4 November 2008, Sciencedaily.com published a story about a research paper in the *National Academy of Sciences*, a very prestigious peer-reviewed scientific journal. The Sciencedaily.com story was headed 'Different roles for mothers and fathers influenced by genetics'.

They reported that researchers from the universities of Exeter and Edinburgh had studied a group of single parents to see how the male single parents did things compared to the female single parents. As a result, the researchers had revealed 'how variation in where males and females put their parenting effort reflects different genetic influences for each sex'. Effectively, these researchers had found that single mothers tended to focus more on directly caring for their children through things like feeding, whereas fathers tended to focus more on indirect caring activities such as keeping the house in order and the preparation of food.

According to the paper's lead author, Professor Allen Moore of the University of Exeter, 'Despite the best efforts of parents to be consistent in child rearing, it is not unusual for mums and dads to differ in the nature of their interactions with offspring ... until recently this was expressed as dad bringing home the bacon and mum taking care of the kids.'

What was really interesting about this study is that the scientists found that there was actually a *genetic* influence on fathers to bring home the bacon and on mothers to take care of the kids, because this pattern of parenting resulted in the parents wanting more children. The research showed that this more traditional division of labour resulted in less conflict between the parents and thus a more efficient family unit.

So, sadly, the feminists had it all wrong. The woman's liberation movement is actually going completely counter to our fundamental genetic code, which leaves the only logical conclusion being that we should all pack up and head back to the '50s.

Compelling stuff, right? I mean, you can't argue with science, and particularly not with genetics, which is only just slightly less sexy than neuroscience.

Let me give you a couple of other facts that – if I were trying to get us all to shift back to the '50s – I might have been a little inclined to leave out on the basis that the whole truth can sometimes be a lot less compelling than a half-truth.

The first is that this particular group of parents has such a strong preference for a particular family size that they will actually kill any children in excess of their preferred number. So, for a start, we're not talking about the most balanced, loving, child-focused parents, are we?

The other point, and it really is quite inconsequential in relation to the rather groundbreaking nature of the study's findings, is that the mothers and fathers in the study were actually beetles. Yes, that's right, beetles. No, not *Beatles* – this wasn't John, Paul, Ringo and George – but actual beetles. *Nicrophorus vespilloides*, a burying beetle from Cornwall, to be precise.

The researchers suggested that their findings could be relevant to other species and even possibly to humans. I think that's a bit of a stretch, and I'm sure a great many other people, and probably a great many scientists, would agree with me, but to be fair they did only say 'possibly' apply to humans.

But do you see how easy it would have been for me to completely slide that one past you as hard scientific fact with huge implications for you and your family? All I would have had to do is leave out the bit about these guys actually being beetles – and probably the bit about them killing their offspring to get their preferred family size – and I could have written a very clever little section completely justifying dads being lazy arses.

I would have been quite safe doing it as well, because I know that the vast majority of people don't go back and check out the research papers for themselves. You would never have known that my grand social plan to move us all back to the 1950s was built on a bunch of infanticidal burying beetles in Cornwall.

I didn't do that, though, because that's not my style. But do you think it's possible that some of the people making all kinds of claims about boys and their brains have done something as sneaky as the one I just tried to slide past you? Surely not.

I mean, they wouldn't tell you a whole lot of stuff about how you should parent your kids and make it sound like it was actual, rock-solid, accepted scientific fact if it was really just a bunch of personal opinions loosely tied to a few studies, some of which were done on whole other species . . . would they?

Digging a little deeper into the 'boy brain'

It turns out that there's quite a bit of stuff we've been told about boys' and girls' brains that smells a little of burying beetles from Cornwall.

Actually, it smells quite a lot of Cornish burying beetles.

In my humble opinion it's *hugely* important that you understand the reality behind many of these statements, because if you have boys, then you're going to hear them.

My wife agreed with me, but she also said I should keep it short and to the point.

'Just because you find all the scientific stuff really interesting doesn't mean everyone does,' she said.

'I know.'

'I mean, this stuff is interesting . . . you just don't want to . . . you know . . . harp on about it.'

'I *know.*'

So in that spirit, let me give you a whistle-stop tour of the major claims being made about boys, and put them in a little more context then you might normally be given.

'Women speak 20,000 words a day and men speak only 7,000.'

Not true.

Really?

Yup.

Are you sure?

Positive.

So where did all that come from, then, because I've heard it a lot?

Actually, variations on this claim have popped up many times over the past several decades. In one of the few studies that has actually been done, researchers used voice-activated tape recorders carried by almost 400 men and women, and they found that, on average, men and women talked the same amount.

So that whole 20,000 versus 7,000 thing was pretty much just made up?

Yup.

'Research shows that newborn girls demonstrate a clear preference for looking at people's faces, whereas boys show a clear preference for looking at moving objects.'

Nope.

Again with the nope?

Yup.

So what's going on?

Well, if you put a baby in a cot and you give it a choice between looking at a picture of a face or looking at a moving mobile, then, on average, some of the baby boys showed a slight preference for looking at the mobile, compared to some of the girls who showed a slight preference for looking at the picture of the face.

That's it?

That's it.

That's hardly convincing.

No, it's not, but it's a good example of something that happens fairly regularly when it comes to gender and neuroscience. The commentators, who hold themselves up as experts, take a slight difference with lots of overlap and turn it into a categorical, black-and-white statement that they then use to justify their opinions.

'Girls' and boys' eyes are hardwired very differently, which is why girls and boys draw different things, and also why girls use lots of colours in their drawings while boys tend to use only a few, darker colours.'

Rats.

Pardon?

Rats.

What do you mean?

A huge amount of that stuff is based on studies of the anatomy of rats' eyes.

You're joking?

Nope.

So people took the difference between male and female rats' eyes and have used that as a basis from which to explain why boys and girls draw different things?

Yes.

That's crazy . . . I mean . . . they're *rats*.

Yes.

Aren't rats nocturnal?

They are.

And would that make a difference?

Could well do.

That really is crazy.

Yes, and in fact even though there *are* very slight differences between male and female humans' eyes, the differences are stronger between ethnic groups than between genders.

So are they going to start suggesting we separate children on the basis of the ethnic make-up of their eyes?

One would hope not.

'Research shows that boys have a disconnection between the emotional centres of their brain and the communication centres of their brain. This is why boys find it hard to talk about their feelings.'

Not really.

Come on, you've got to be kidding? That stuff sounds pretty bloody convincing.

It might sound convincing, but that doesn't mean it's true.

So what's the deal?

Statements like that can typically be traced back to a study done in 2001 on a grand total of 19 kids.

So what did they do in this study?

They showed the kids pictures of the faces of people who looked afraid and took fMRI pictures of their brains to see what happened when they looked at the faces.

Sounds pretty cool.

Yes it does, but the study had all kinds of limitations.

Such as?

Well, aside from *all* the technical limitations when you're taking brain scans of people looking at pictures and trying to say how that applies to the real world, there were only 19 kids.

So what?

If you have only 19 kids, then any one kid can really skew the results.

Is that a big deal?

It's a very big deal.

Basically, what you're saying is that people have taken one small piece of research and made huge statements about what that research means, which the research doesn't actually confirm?

That's exactly what I'm saying.

'Girls' hearing is about seven times more sensitive than boys' hearing, so boys tend not to hear softly spoken female teachers.'

Now you're going to tell me that's not true either?

No.

So it *is* true?

It's kind- of true.

What do you mean?

A lot of very complex arguments have gone on around this one, but it seems that when you peel it all apart, you get left with the position that while girls might have slightly more sensitive hearing than boys, it's likely to be so slight that it won't make any real difference.

But, if you'll excuse the pun, I've heard this one a lot, so doesn't that mean there must be something to it?

Again, just because you hear something a lot doesn't mean that it's actually true.

'Depending on who you listen to, brain scans have shown that boys' brain development is anywhere from 6 months to 2.5 years behind girls when they start school.'

That's a right Dover train station, that is, Guv'ner.

Pardon?

Dover train station. It's cockney rhyming slang for 'over-interpretation'.

Oh, why's that, then?

There have been studies that have shown differences between the brain scans of boys and girls, but the problem is that they are small average differences with lots of individual variation.

Which means?

It means that while there might be a small average difference between the boy scans and the girl scans when you compare them as a group, there can be so much individual variation between boys, and between girls, that the average comparisons of the two groups as a whole are a bit meaningless.

Oh, so the brain-scan stuff isn't clear-cut?

Not at all. In fact, there are all kinds of problems when you're trying to make actual statements about real-world stuff based on brain scans.

So how does this whole brain scan thing work anyway?

Well, it's complicated, and not everyone is interested in that stuff, so I'm going to do that in a separate box so that people who find technical stuff boring can just skip it and get on with their lives.

Sure, but you're not making sexist assumptions about women and science are you?

Not all, but I am making the assumption that not everyone finds the maths and physics of fMRI scans as interesting as I do.

Oh, fair enough.

Brain scans –
all you ever need to know
to look clever at dinner parties

Mostly when people talk about brain scans, they are talking about an fMRI, or functional Magnetic Resonance Imaging. There are all kinds of ways that scientists study the brain (here we go alphabet-crazy:

PET, EEG, sMRI, MRS and DTI), but because fMRI is one of the most commonly used techniques, I thought I'd give you a quick rundown of the issues just with this technique so you can get your head around how difficult this stuff is.

How fMRI works is that you put a given person inside a really big, really expensive machine, and it clicks and whirs and bangs for a bit. The end result of all the clicking, whirring and banging is that a computer produces an image of what is happening in that person's brain.

Except, here's the complex bit (although let's be honest, the whole bloody thing seems pretty complex to most of us): it doesn't take a picture of neurons (brain cells) firing; instead, it measures brain activity indirectly by getting an electronic measure of changes in blood oxygenation called a BOLD (blood oxygenation level-dependent) signal. The rationale is that the more the brain cells are firing, the more blood oxygenation will change. The fMRI then turns these activation signals into 'voxels', small 3D cubes ($<3mm^3$), which are like the pixels on your digital camera.

So while it doesn't measure brain cell activity directly, the fMRI does it in a sneakily indirect way by measuring the BOLD signal, the stuff that changes as brain cells are firing, and turning that into the fMRI equivalent of a pixel, which for reasons we don't need to know about they call a voxel. The more the brain cells fire, the more the blood oxygenation will change, and so the stronger the activation signal will be, and the stronger the voxel on the final image will be.

That's pretty clever.

Yes, indeedy.

So what this means is that we now are able to make all kinds of statements about how people's brains work, because we just get them to do stuff and then look at our nice little voxel-based picture of the brain?

Well, no, not really.

Oh.

Yeah.

So how come it isn't that simple?

It turns out, sadly, that there are a number of problems with making definitive statements based on fMRI pictures of the brain. It isn't just as simple as measuring the BOLD signals through a pretty pattern of voxels in a part of the fMRI scan that then tells us exactly how brains work.

Bummer.

Yeah, it's a bummer alright.

Is there some simple, not quite so drawn-out way of explaining why that is?

Sure there is: bullet points. Let me give you the fundamentals of why we need to be very careful in deciding what fMRI images (commonly called 'brain scans' in the media) are actually telling us:

◇ The most basic problem is that you can't test abilities in the real-world settings. People are tested while they're lying inside a machine, so that's going to create problems generalising back to actual abilities in the real world.

◇ The BOLD signal can change based on the part of the brain being examined, the type of task or stimulus being used, the age and health of the person being scanned and whether or not they've had caffeine or nicotine (although you'd hope that this last factor wouldn't be a common issue with kids). Basically, it's pretty variable.

◇ On top of all that, BOLD signals may also be different in the same person at different times, making it hard to establish a 'baseline'.

◇ Sometimes the part of the brain that is of interest may be too small for the pattern of voxels to stand out. Scientists are currently working on fMRIs that will be able to get the voxel down to $1mm^3$, which will greatly help, but we aren't there just yet.

◇ We still don't know how BOLD signals are influenced by developing areas of the brain in children. Some studies have shown that there are similarities between the BOLD signals of children and adults, but there are still a lot of things that need to be worked out before we can make any definitive statements about what fMRI scans of children really mean.

◇ The statistics used to analyse the results are really complicated. There are lots of examples in the research literature where arguments break out because one group of researchers says that another group of researchers haven't got the maths right and so their results aren't what they thought they were.

The big message in all of this for all of us is that the 'brain-scan' stuff we hear so much about isn't as cut-and-dried as it's sometimes painted to be. There are more claims about what fMRIs have 'proven' than I've had hot dinners, and there will no doubt be many more to come. I'm not saying it's all rubbish, because a machine that costs something in the vicinity of $3 million has to be doing something pretty clever; what I *am* saying is that we need to be a little cautious before we leap to a whole bunch of assumptions about what these images are telling us about ourselves, and particularly about our boys.

Perhaps it's best to let an actual scientist, Dr John T Bruer (and admittedly, he's written extensively about his scepticism regarding the claims often made about the implications of neuroscience for the real world), sum this one up:

If neuroscientists are to prevent their work from being misrepresented, they must think more critically about how their research is presented to educators and the public, and in particular they must be very cautious about even the most innocent speculation about the practical significance of basic research. They should remind the interested public that we are just at the beginning of our scientific enquiry into how neural structures implement mental functions and how mental functions guide behaviour.

The thing about fMRI-based research, if you were to boil it right down to fat and bone, is that unless you're very rigorous in how you design, run, analyse, interpret and talk about your study, there's a pretty big risk that anything you say may contain the macroscopic footprints of legions of Cornish burying beetles.

Take-home messages

There is no doubt that studies of how our brains function have contributed greatly to our understanding of what makes us do the things we do. Equally, there is no doubt that in the coming years we will learn things about the wrinkly grey blob between our ears that will change the way we think about ourselves, and each other. The trick, though, is not to try to run before we've even put our shoes on.

What I've tried to do in this chapter is show you that some of the bold statements being made about the differences between men's and women's brains are nowhere near as solid as they might first appear. The reason it's so important to understand this stuff is that once these claims are thrown around enough, they achieve the status of truth without sometimes being completely true.

Scientists have observed *some* differences in male and female brains, but these tend to be small, and clouded in all kinds of issues that make definitive statements about what they mean all but impossible. However, as we've seen, this hasn't stopped some people from going ahead and making incredibly definitive statements anyway.

My hope is that this chapter will help you to be more critical of the next new, amazing 'scientific' claim about boys you read about in the newspaper or see on the telly. Important people are debating this stuff, and they're making policy decisions that will affect both your boys and mine, sometimes based on theories predicated on little more than the behaviour of Cornish burying beetles.

So question the things you're told about your boy – *including* the things I tell you. A bit of healthy scepticism is always a good thing.

9

The bit where I eat a slice of freshly baked humble pie

The worst thing of all, at least for me anyway, was that when I started researching this book I discovered that I'd been guilty of this very thing myself. I'd unwittingly quoted weak science in one of *my* books as if it were fact. Needless to say, I blushed. The discovery that I'd been suckered in to pushing the hype just like everybody else was more than a little humbling, and just a little embarrassing.

So because I think it's important to practise what you preach, and because it's important to our current conversation, I give you the following section clarifying a dumb thing that I've said as an example of how good intentions mixed with a lack of cross-checking can end in tears.

When I wrote *Before Your Teenagers Drive You Crazy, Read This!* one of the things that I really wanted to provide people with was a good, clear, practical explanation of the startling changes that take place in teenagers' brains. There actually are startling changes, and they really do have a significant impact on how teenagers feel, think and act. My view has always been that if you have a way of understanding why they do what they do, it makes it all a little easier to deal with. I've had a lot of emails from people who've said that they found that stuff very helpful, which is gratifying.

The problem was that in a section called 'Girls have broadband' I talk about the corpus callosum, the bundle of fibres that connects the left and right sides of the brain, and the differences between girls and boys. In that section, I said the following:

> It turns out that the female corpus callosum is 30% thicker than that of boys. Now, even though it doesn't look great to have an exclamation point right after a percentage sign, I think this situation warrants it. So here goes: 30%!
>
> Let's stop and think about the implications of this for just a moment. The corpus callosum is the bridge between the two halves of the brain that channels information from one side to the other. What this means is that the systems within an average teenage girl's brain are going to be able to work as a far more effective tag-wrestling team. With girls' brains you're not just facing a single-file system of troublemakers – you're facing a gang, *en masse*, communicating with a high-speed internet connection.

While it might be a zippy little metaphor, and even though it might seem to have some grounding in many parents' experience of their teenage daughters, it is in fact a very long way from being an accurate statement. On closer inspection, I discovered that this statement was covered in the droppings of a certain beetle, our old friend *Nicrophorus vespilloides*.

Bugger.

It was only in writing and researching *this* book, and digging a little deeper to try to understand how the myth of the boy crisis was created – and indeed how it has shaped and continues to shape some of the scientific dialogue – that I felt the need to go back and check a little more thoroughly the things I'd said about boys' and girls' brains, in light of what I was learning about the politics of sex differences.

I didn't make up the 30% figure: it came from an article in a peer-reviewed scientific journal. It seemed pretty convincing when I read it, too, and it seemed to explain something I'd seen in the real world myself, so I put it in the book.

It was more than a little crushing to discover that in fact there have been a number of studies that have actually found that there is *no* difference between the relative size of the corpus callosum in men and women. It turns out that this 30% figure, and a number of variations on it, have been given credible status because somewhere along the way it started being bandied about without any detailed fact-checking.

If it sounds good, we believe it.

Now, while I said before it's a bit embarrassing to make a mistake like that, my view has always been that if you make a gaff then it's best to fess up and put things right as soon as you can. Learn from it, take the offending piece of pop-neuroscience gobbledygook out of future editions and move on. If the science doesn't fit your theory, then you need to adjust your theory.

Unfortunately, as we've seen, not everyone thinks the same way.

10

The crisis in boys' education – or is there?

When I was a young lad, going to school was a fairly uncomplicated process. I got up, had breakfast, packed my wee bag and off I went. Simple. My mum and dad chose my school on the sole basis that it was the one at the end of the road. They didn't go on the internet and do any research; not only because there was no internet then, but mainly because it would have seemed a bit daft. I mean, there's a school just down the end of the street. What else do you need to know? They didn't even ask around. They just pointed and said: 'That way.'

I even went to a single-sex high school. Again, not out of choice, or because my parents were driven by any particular ideological stance; it was simply the only high school in town. We didn't have a co-ed option. The boys' school had been there for the better part of a hundred years and so off I went.

Nowadays, as with just about everything else, it's a little more complicated. The whole issue of boys and schooling has become a bit of a hot potato, and has provoked a great deal of heated debate and discussion. There's an awful lot of referencing to statistics that goes on, and it seems like everyone has an agenda.

I have my own very clear agenda as well, because I'm the father of two boys. I have an utterly personal stake in trying to untangle all the rhetoric and the numbers to try to figure out what the best options are for boys when it comes to education, because, just like you, I want to make the best decisions for my boys based on the facts and not some underlying ideology. I'm interested in finding out how boys are *really* doing in school, the whole single-sex versus co-ed debate, and most importantly what can we all do to give our boys the best shot at getting a good education.

Like I said, this is a hot issue and so what I'm going to try to do here is give you as balanced an appraisal of the state of the game as I possibly can. Also, just so you know, in Part Four I'm going to go into all the practical stuff about how you as a parent can help your boy do his best in school. The usual caveats apply, though, because even though I'm going to do my best to give you a balanced view of this whole thing, it's still going to end up being my opinion, so keep that in mind is all I'm saying.

How are boys doing in school?

We're increasingly hearing that there is a crisis in boys' education, and the evidence given to support this view is that boys are consistently shown to be lagging behind girls in school performance, and that universities are filling up with girls while boys fall by the wayside.

Is that true? Well, kind of.

The most commonly reported finding from a number of quite large studies in a number of countries over the past several decades is that boys lag behind girls in reading and writing, and that boys do better in maths and physical sciences. Actually it's even grimmer than that for boys, because now girls have caught up in the area of maths as well. The evidence for this is taken from average differences in reading, writing and maths scores, the higher prevalence of reading disabilities in boys, and enrolment rates in tertiary education.

Just as an example: if you look at the proportion of boys enrolling in college in the United States between 1949 and 2006, it looks a little alarming.

1949 — 70%	1989 — 46%
1959 — 64%	1999 — 44%
1969 — 59%	2006 — 42%
1979 — 49%	

At first I found this all a little depressing, because it seemed that my own boys were destined for a life of ditch-digging because the girls were going to get all the best grades in school. Not only were my boys apparently going to perform poorly in school, but it seemed that even if they did make it as far as university, they would find the campus awash with girls who would, once again, outperform them there as well. (Actually, I think that if a guy turned up at university at age 18 and found it awash with girls, he'd probably be pretty damn happy, but that's a whole other argument.)

All this was a bit of a puzzle, because there have been a huge number of studies that have looked at basic cognitive ability in boys compared to girls (that is, how smart boys and girls are) and they've all found that there is no real difference. There are tiny average differences on particular abilities, but nothing of any real functional significance.

So if boys are just as smart as girls, why are girls consistently outperforming boys in school, why are more boys than girls diagnosed with reading disabilities, and why are more girls going on to university than boys?

Possible causes

There are three major possibilities that are often suggested as causes for this observed difference between girls and boys:

biological or 'hardwiring' differences; the increasing feminisation of schools; and gender-based personality differences. I'm going to quickly cover these off, because you will almost certainly come up against this stuff at some point during your boy's school career.

'Boys are "hardwired" differently'

Here we come up against all the old chestnuts we first met in Chapter 6, which is all the stuff about how boys can't hear as well as girls, their eyes are hardwired differently and their brains develop differently than girls' brains. These arguments are used as the 'scientific basis' for why boys need to be taught differently to girls, and hence why we should have single-sex schools.

We'll get to the single-sex versus co-ed schools debate a little later in this chapter, and I've already talked about the hearing and the eyes and how those claims are just ever so slightly exaggerated, but let me just explain very briefly the argument around the different brain-development stuff, because that's now being used by people advocating that boys should actually start school at six so that their brains are ready to go.

The gist of the argument is that, based on the definitive results of the largest study of developing brains conducted in the past five years, if boys start school at age five then they won't be able to read as well as girls because their brains aren't sufficiently developed to learn to read, and therefore they will lag behind and hate reading.

Does this mean we should all rush out and drag our five-year-old boys out of school least we instil in them a mortal loathing of reading? No, we shouldn't.

Once again, with a little digging – although it wasn't even digging really, it was more like blowing a little loose dirt off the top – things are not quite that definitive. The recommendation that boys start school a year later than girls is largely based on a study from the NIMH (National Institute of Mental Health) in the United States, which looked at the MRI scans of 387 individuals ranging in age from 3 to 27 years. They *did* find differences in the brain development of boys and girls, and it included findings that growth in the frontal portion of the brain peaked in girls at 10.5 years and 11.5 years for boys, which all sounds pretty damn conclusive. I mean, you know, that clearly shows that boys' brains and girls' brains develop along different trajectories, which means the claims that boys should start school a year later and be taught differently are completely justified. Right?

Well, not really, because – among a whole bunch of really complicated qualifiers and notes of caution about the implications of their results – the authors of the study also made the following, *slightly* important general qualifier:

> Differences in brain sizes between males and females should not be interpreted as implying any functional advantage or disadvantage.

Huh? You mean they actually say the results they found shouldn't be taken as saying anything in particular about how girls and boys actually function?

That's right. The study's authors made a point of saying that, even though what they'd found was both interesting and potentially significant, everyone should be a little cautious before they read too much into it. There were a whole lot of issues that made it too difficult to say anything definitive about *function* based on their observations of *structural* differences.

So does it say *anything* in there about boys and when they should start school?

Nope, the researchers don't make *any* statements *anywhere* in the article about what this might mean in terms of schooling for boys and girls. They certainly don't suggest that we start boys in school a year later than girls based on their findings. If you want to read the paper for yourself, you'll find a reference at the back of this book in the endnotes so you can go find it yourself on the internet. I strongly suggest that you don't just take my word for it, but go have a look for yourself.

Sooner or later someone's going to throw that brain-development line at you, so I think it's really important you know what that particular claim is based on . . . or *not* based on, as the case may be. My boys both started school at age five. They can both read, and what's more they both enjoy reading. So again, while I'm sure there are some differences in the hardwiring of boys and girls, it doesn't look like that's actually able to explain why girls tend to do better at school than boys.

'The feminisation of schools'

I have to admit that I fell for this one for a while. I'm a little ashamed to admit it, but it's true. The argument goes that because the education system is now largely run by women, masculine values have been replaced by feminine values. The result of this is that schools have developed a feminine culture that is hostile towards boys. In this feminised environment, 'normal' boy behaviour is seen as 'bad' and so boys are constrained to behave in ways that are completely foreign to them. Hey presto – boys failing in schools.

And what's the obvious answer?

Get more males back into schools, pump up the masculine culture stuff – and, hey anti-presto, we'll get it all sorted.

It's like I was saying way back in Chapter 3, we don't sift information in a neutral and rational fashion, we tend to see what we want to see. This whole notion of the feminisation of schools struck a bit of a chord all over the place, and educators and politicians alike were all charging around busily trying to recruit men back into teaching to address the issue. The hope was that if we had more male teachers, then boys' performance in school would start to improve.

Once again, with a little digging it seemed that the rhetoric wasn't actually based on all that much fact. Conversely, the facts themselves seemed to prove pretty conclusively that having a male teacher or a female teacher didn't, in and of itself, make *any* difference to the outcomes for students. For example, a study of 413 separate classes for 11-year-olds in England (113 taught by males and 300 taught by females) found there was 'no discernible impact' on the learning outcomes of boys or girls. As another example, a Dutch study that involved 163 schools, 251 teachers and 5,181 pupils found that the teacher's gender had 'no effect whatsoever on the achievement, attitudes or behaviour of pupils', and that this was true for both boys and girls, and held true for culture and socio-economic status.

One reason for that might be that male and female teachers' behaviour in the classroom doesn't actually differ along gender lines. The traditional (and just ever-so-slightly sexist) generalisation would be that male teachers would tend to be stricter, while female teachers would tend to be a bit more lax. In an interesting study, researchers observed 51 separate classes in English schools (25 male teachers and 26 female teachers), and analysed how they spoke to, and interacted with, their classes. They found that, rather than being split along male and female lines, teachers fell into one of two groups: disciplinarian or liberal teaching style. This wasn't determined by gender, but was more a matter of personal style.

And, when you think about it, haven't teachers always asked pupils to sit still and be quiet? I could be remembering things a little differently, but I'm pretty sure when I was at school we had to sit still and be quiet, and I'm pretty sure the same was true of my mum and dad when they were at school as well.

So it seems that – at least in terms of educational achievement, attitude, and behaviour – it doesn't make any difference for boys whether or not they have a male or a female teacher. It also seems like the stereotypes that we have about female teachers and their 'feminised classrooms' don't seem to be all that accurate either. There may be more female teachers in schools than in days gone by, but, despite the vast amount of hoo-ha about feminised schools, that doesn't seem to be a problem.

Actually, there's another big message here specifically for mums as well. If you think about the teacher as a role model (and also as a surrogate parent figure during the day), female teachers are just as good for boys as male teachers. You see where I'm leading? Boys respond just as well to female role models as they do to male role models. Store that away for now and we'll come back to it in a later chapter.

'Cotton Wool Syndrome'

It has long been a personal worry of mine that in the often ridiculous extremes we go to to keep children safe, we are sucking all the fun out of children's worlds. Nowhere is this more obvious than at school. Playgrounds look great, but they're all a bit soft. All the fun stuff has gone, and we've replaced it with brightly coloured, very nice-looking, but slightly insipid playground equipment. The rope bridges that used to be 3 metres off the ground are now 30 centimetres off the ground. Even the ground isn't the ground anymore; instead, it's invariably bouncy rubber surfaces.

What's more, the nature of how we let children play has changed as well. The traditional rough games of the past have been outlawed and replaced instead with . . . well, to be honest, I'm not sure. Gone is British bulldogs in many schools. Gone, too, are dodgeball and full-contact sport. There are schools in New Zealand and Australia, and I'm sure elsewhere in the world, where children aren't allowed to run. You know, just in case. There are also schools where children aren't allowed to touch each other. You know, just in case.

Worse still, we've abandoned the notion of competition in case it damages the self-esteem of anyone who doesn't come first.

Now we *all* come first. So you might be a really talented athlete, who actually goes out and trains and works hard, but if you come first in a race at school you will get no more recognition than the bloke who came last because he eats too many pies.

And the 'zero tolerance for violence' stuff has become almost ridiculous in many places. This is particularly difficult for boys, whose games often include people being shot, stabbed, speared, blown up and decapitated. All this is ripping good fun, but would be frowned upon greatly in many schools.

This is not so much about the 'feminisation' of schools in my opinion, but is more about the overcautiousness of schools or 'Cotton Wool Syndrome'. Most of the Western world has become so incredibly risk-averse that we have taken all the fun stuff away from children, and from boys in particular. We can't just blame those 'pesky boy-hating feminists' for this, because men have actually been in charge quite a lot of the time that this has gone on. We're *all* to blame for letting this happen.

Now, I don't know if this has an impact on boys' learning, but I do believe it's made schools, and life in general, a little less fun. It seems a little obvious to me that if you have more fun at school, you're probably going to want to be there more, and maybe even to learn more. All of this raises the question: Is the real problem maybe that boys just don't fit into the school environment quite so well as girls? As we'll see next, it turns out I wasn't the first person to consider that possibility.

'Personality differences between boys and girls may explain their different performance in school'

I was talking with one of my clients one day about her observations of the boys in her son's class. She tested them on a list of words they'd been given to remember and then marked them off on a list, much as parent helpers do in classrooms all over the world.

'Boys are so different to girls,' she said.

'How so?' I asked.

'Well, when you ask the girls to come over to do their words, they just do, and then they sit down quietly and get on with it.'

'And the boys?'

She rolled her eyes, 'They jiggle about and say silly things and are generally just a lot harder to get to focus on things.'

'Why do you think that is?' I asked.

She shrugged. 'They're boys.'

Her observations of the boys' behaviour are pretty darned relevant to what we're talking about here, because boys and girls do act quite differently in school. You don't have to be a rocket scientist to see this if you spend any amount of time in a schoolyard. Boys tend to rush around and yell at each other, and the girls tend to gather together in clumps and talk. It's a stereotype to be sure, but it's a stereotype that mirrors pretty closely the actual behaviour in most of the schoolyards I've ever seen.

This is one of the reasons that differences in personality have been suggested as a cause of the boy–girl achievement gap. Maybe girls are somehow just better suited to the school environment?

There have been a number of studies that have looked at how personality factors influence school performance in boys, and what they've found so far is quite interesting. It seems that, for boys, liking what they're doing is more important than it is for girls. When you stop and think about the fact that a lot of the stuff you learn in school is inherently dull, clearly just this alone is going to favour girls if they are more able to get on with doing stuff they find boring.

I remember getting bored almost to the point of brain embolism in maths in high school. I did not then, nor do I now, know or care about how to multiply vectors. In fact, I can't even do long division without a calculator, and again this is not because it's beyond me – I just don't care. I have never had to do long division to save my life or avoid serious injury, and have never heard of anyone who has; hence, I don't see the relevance of it for me. I will undoubtedly go to my grave without ever having grasped even the basics of working with vectors.

So, yeah, I'd agree that for boys it's important to enjoy what you're supposed to be learning.

What is also interesting is that, while boys tend to be less anxiety-prone in relation to school in general, when they are anxious it has a much bigger impact than it does for girls. So it seems that boys don't panic as much as girls at a general level, but, for those boys who do get stressed, they tend to lose the plot more than girls.

One study that I also found quite interesting was an investigation into the studying habits of boys and girls. Researchers in England looked at a sample of 310 Year 10 and Year 11 high-achieving pupils from two single-sex schools. They found that the boys did less homework than the girls, but paradoxically the boys got better grades. What this says is that these boys had better studying habits than the girls, because they did less homework but achieved better results.

I felt that my whole approach to my university studies had been vindicated by that one piece of research. Early on in my academic career I had elected to focus not so much on *actual* learning, but more on trying to predict what would be in the exams and then to just learn that. As a result I spent a lot of time analysing exam papers for patterns and trying to calculate the odds of a given question being asked. Generally, that strategy has worked out pretty well for me. It also might help to explain why some boys seem to do really well in school with very little work. This often drives their mums crazy, because they can't understand why their sons don't just knuckle down and work really hard.

Strategy. It's all about strategy.

What does seem pretty clear from the personality research is that boy culture is not as school-friendly as girl culture. This probably explains why boys tend to get into trouble more, and why far more boys than girls end up on special behavioural programmes. Whether or not this constitutes a crisis is up for debate. I rather suspect that boys have always got into more trouble at school than girls. Again and again I keep coming back to the conclusion that the 'gap' between boys and girls is not so much about boys failing out of a hostile, boy-hating system, but just that girls are improving at a faster rate.

In any case, it does seem that the more research people do in this area, the more we may learn about how boys and girls approach school differently. The personality stuff rings a little more true for me. It fits more with what I see in boys and girls at school than more fanciful notions of different brains or feminised schools. At the very least, it's the one area where the existing science is actually knocking up against real differences.

Yet somehow it didn't feel quite right to leave it there. The numbers did look kind of grim, and for a while that made me a little anxious (*Darn those pesky higher-achieving girls*, I found myself muttering into the piles of research articles I was reading). But then I thought to myself, well hang on, so far I've found quite a few things that looked pretty damning at first glance when it comes to boys, and with a little digging I've found it wasn't quite as grim as things first appeared. Maybe I should dig a little deeper?

So I dug a little deeper

I just want to take you back a minute to the often-quoted basis of the alleged crisis in boys' education. Recall that this 'call to arms' to save boys from ending up with the short end of the education stick is based on the numbers of boys going through to university/college, the higher rates of reading disabilities diagnosed in boys and their lower scores on tests of reading and mathematics.

So let's look at all that a little closer.

'Fewer boys are going to university/college'

One of the things that we're told you can't argue with is the numbers. Numbers don't lie, we're told, so all you have to do is look at the numbers and you'll find the truth. You can't argue with the fact that the proportion of boys on campuses in many countries in the world is shrinking. Recall the stats for the United States, for example:

1949 — 70%	1989 — 46%
1959 — 64%	1999 — 44%
1969 — 59%	2006 — 42%
1979 — 49%	

Can't argue with that, right?

Well, no, but I have to say that I'm a little confused about when the education division of the 'boy crisis' is supposed to have started? Because if you look at those figures, then you'd have to say that things started going sour for boys as far back as the 1950s. So does that mean the world started becoming a more hostile place for boys 60 years ago? And if so, what the hell's that about? Some great social conspiracy hatched by the feminists all those years ago?

So then I started wondering if there was another way of looking at those figures. What if you simply re-wrote the figures as the percentage of *girls* going on to higher education?

1949 — 30%	1989 — 64%
1959 — 36%	1999 — 66%
1969 — 41%	2006 — 68%
1979 — 51%	

Hmmm. Maybe it isn't so much about boys doing *worse*, as it is about girls doing *better*? I'm not the first one to suggest this, of course, because others have voiced similar thoughts before.

It doesn't seem that radical an idea to me, because what we do know is that since 1949 there has been a continuing move towards equality between the sexes. It seems to me that all that's been happening is that boys have been plodding along as they always have, and girls, for all the reasons we talked about in the previous section, have simply picked up the ball and run with it.

'More boys than girls are diagnosed with reading disabilities'

The first time I heard this was quite some time ago on telly. One of the 'boy crisis' advocates said it, and I remember thinking that it was both troubling and strange. Troubling, because more boys were being diagnosed with reading disabilities, which is clearly not good; and strange, because more *boys* were being diagnosed with reading disabilities. I remember wondering at the time why more boys were being diagnosed with reading disabilities and not more *children* generally?

I concluded that there were only two conceivable explanations. The first is that those pesky feminists were obviously contaminating the drinking water with brain-altering drugs that were both non-detectable and only affected male brains. The second is that there must be something off about the way we were testing or measuring reading abilities that made boys seem worse than they really were.

To test these theories, I staked out our local city reservoir for several weeks. I cleverly constructed a forward OP (or 'observation post', for those of you who don't watch SAS videos on YouTube), and laid up in such a way that I could surreptitiously observe feminist activity without being seen. Apart from a lady out jogging with what appeared to be a poodle crossed with a small horse, I was not able to observe any sneaky feminist activity. At that point, after 36 days of living rough in the bush, and observing no water-tampering activities implicating the feminists, I concluded that there must be something off about the testing procedure and went home for a shower and a hot cup of tea.

What I didn't know then – and I wish I had, because 36 days hiding in scrub watching a water reservoir is not a fun way to spend a month – is that an Israeli and a Kiwi (not the bird obviously, but an actual person from New Zealand) had already figured out a major part of that particular puzzle.

Using data from a longitudinal study that has been following over 900 children for the past 35 years, two researchers discovered an interesting and potentially incredibly important error in the way we measure how well kids can read. It's a complicated statistical thing, but in a nutshell it boils down to this:

◊ There is a statistically based gender bias in how we predict how well kids should read.

◊ Because of this statistical bias, we *overestimate* benchmarks for how well we think boys should read, and *underestimate* the benchmarks for how well girls should read.

◊ This means that more boys fail to reach these benchmarks, and so more boys get diagnosed as having a reading disability.

◊ It also means that more girls who do have a reading disability are shown as being OK when they really should be diagnosed as having a reading disability.

◊ When the statistical glitch was corrected, the researchers found that girls and boys ended up with the same levels of reading disabilities.

Wow, so are you saying girls may be just as reading-disabled as boys?

Well, there's certainly grounds for a little caution around those particular statistics.

You know, all this is starting to make the whole boy crisis thing sound a little overstated, don't you think?

I do.

So you think the pesky feminists had anything to do with jacking up the scores so boys seem worse than they are?

Undoubtedly.

What can we do about it?

Well, I'm going to set up a forward OP and stake out some testing centres.

So, is there anything else we should know?

Yup.

Is that the next section then? The one titled 'Not everybody thinks boys are doing that badly'?

Yup.

Not everybody thinks boys are doing that badly

When almost everything you read talks about the emerging 'boy crisis' in education in most developed nations, and when you repeatedly hear about how the reading test scores and maths test scores are all saying that boys are in trouble, it's easy to see how you could start to believe that boys are in trouble. A few people have suggested that boys are not in trouble, and that in fact there is research that suggests things may not be quite so dire, but they generally get rubbished as being part of the feminist conspiracy for total world domination.

I decided to dig a little deeper myself to see what I could find. As I was clicking through an online service that lets you search through papers in scientific journals, I saw an article entitled 'The mythical "boy crisis"'. I clicked the link, and then another link, closed the whole thing by mistake, cursed, logged back on, searched again, found it, clicked on the right link this time and found myself reading a pretty interesting scientific article.

Two researchers had decided that they'd quite like to see if the education 'boy crisis' was as bad as everyone was saying. To do that, they designed a large study with over 17,500 children in

994 schools in the United States. So, you know, it was a *lot* of kids in a *lot* of schools.

And what did they find?

◇ White boys outperformed white girls in maths across virtually the entire distribution by the end of the first year of school.

◇ White boys gained ground generally across the first years of school.

◇ Black and Hispanic boys gained ground in only certain areas.

◇ Boys lagged behind girls in reading at the start of kindergarten and at the end of the first three years of school.

◇ Only the lowest-achieving students lost ground over the first four years of school.

◇ Boys gained ground in reading between the first and third years of school.

Now, the important thing to understand here is not the specifics, but the bigger message. It isn't *all* boys who are in trouble, but *some* boys. In fact, this pattern emerges all over the place, because once you start to separate out race from gender, then you start to see that it isn't a global problem for *boys*, but in fact it's more a problem for particular ethnic groups. And just to be clear, this isn't about differences in baseline intelligence or abilities between different ethnic groups, but socio-economic differences in access to resources.

If you spend any time at all looking at the data on achievement in schools, it's pretty obvious you can build the story almost any way you want, and various people have done just that on both sides of the argument. I think the picture says that it's not a cut-and-dried issue that *all* boys are in trouble. I think the picture says that *some* boys are in trouble. In any case, once again I don't think that for us as parents it really matters what the big picture is. The 'average level of achievement for boys in reading' won't affect your boy's ability to read at all.

But you can.

Single-sex versus co-ed schools

This is the Ground Zero of the 'boy crisis' education debate. This is where the ideologically based 'interpretations' of the science start to pile up in great big clumpy heaps. Which is why you need to be wearing suitably well-informed wellies, because this is where it all gets a bit muddy. Just to recap, the major reasons usually given by those advocating that boys must be educated separately to girls are as follows.

◊ Boys' brains develop more slowly, and in a different pattern than girls' brains.
Reality: This statement is a gross overinterpretation of the science.

◊ Boys' hearing is less sensitive than girls' hearing.
Reality: While boys' hearing may be slightly less sensitive than girls', the difference is unlikely to be significant or even noticeable.

◊ Boys' visual systems are hardwired differently.
Reality: Another gross overinterpretation of the science. There are bigger ethnically based differences between our eyes than gender-based differences.

◊ There are personality differences between boys and girls that mean they approach school and learning very differently.
Reality: That's correct at a general level, but again there are large individual differences between children, irrespective of gender.

The big question for all of us as parents is obviously whether or not there is any evidence that single-sex schools are inherently better for boys than co-ed schools. Is there something about a single-sex school that makes it a better option for boys than a co-ed school?

Having had a bit of a trawl around the internet and visited the websites of various organisations advocating for single-sex education, I was left with the very clear impression that it was a total no-brainer. All the research that was quoted seemed to show fairly convincingly that there is a sizeable advantage for boys in attending a single-sex school.

Then I thought that maybe I should go check the research out for myself, just to be safe, given that we've seen so far that some of these people have a tendency to bend the science to fit their theories.

While you can find studies that conclude single-sex schools are better for boys than co-ed schools, there is almost always a raft of qualifying factors. These often include things like socio-economic differences between boys' schools (which tend to be private) and co-ed schools (which tend to be public). What we know is that boys from higher socio-economic brackets do better than boys in the lower socio-economic brackets. When researchers have done clever statistical things to cancel out the effects of things like socio-economic status and other potentially confounding variables, they have found that the performance differences largely disappear.

Now, I have no doubt that you can get on the internet and find people quoting research that does show a clear advantage for boys in single-sex education, and I've got no doubt some of the single-sex schooling defenders will email me papers showing just that. What I also am in no doubt about, however, is that the picture is far from the definitive 'interpretation' of the research that some people are putting out.

Once again, the best we seem able to say is that *some* boys do better in *some* single-sex schools than *some* boys in *some* co-ed schools. The reverse is also the case, though, because *some* boys in co-ed schools do better than *some* boys in single-sex schools.

You might be thinking about now that I'm against single-sex schools, but actually I'm not. I've seen some fantastic single-sex schools, so I'm not opposed to the idea on any kind of ideological basis. The thing is I'm not inherently in favour of them either. The fact that a given school is single-sex or co-ed is of no consequence to me. What I *am* in favour of, and strongly advocate for, are *good* schools, regardless of what the composition of the students is. I think that you should make the decision about which school to send your boys to based on what you think is best for them, not on what other people tell you is best for them. Having spent many years working with many different kinds of schools, it's my view that trying to make any kind of global statements about what types of schools are best for all boys is just silly. There are a *huge* number of factors that influence how well boys do in school, as is also true for girls, and so a one-size-fits-all approach is bound to miss the mark for many boys. It has long been my experience that one of the most fundamentally important factors in the success or otherwise of a school lies in the leadership abilities of the head teacher and senior staff. A good head teacher generally means you have a good school.

The two most important factors for success in school

Encouragingly, there are some things that the researchers *do* seem to agree on; two things, in fact. When you strip away all the controversy, and competing claims, and debate, there does appear to be good agreement on what the two most important factors are for success in school:

◊ intelligence

◊ self-esteem

This might seem a little obvious, but then in my experience most things are. Of all the thousands of studies, of hundreds of thousands of kids around the world, the two factors that have been demonstrated time and again to have the biggest impact on how boys (and girls) perform in school are intelligence and self-esteem – how smart you are, and how good you feel about yourself.

So what does this mean for mums raising boys?

Without wishing to seem cold, the first thing is to make babies with the smartest guys you can find. After that, it isn't really about playing Baby Mozart tapes or buying 'brain-building' toys so much as it is about warm, consistent care. There is now pretty good evidence that, for the great majority of us, our baseline intelligence remains pretty stable over the course of our lives. We might learn more stuff, but the basic computing power remains the same. The best start we can give our kids is to provide them with a safe environment, good nutrition and warm, consistent care. The more relaxed and happy kids are, the better they will fare later in life.

Obviously there isn't a lot you can do about the genes your child inherits, but you can do quite a bit to make the environment they grow up in a nurturing and brain-friendly place. This doesn't mean that if you yell at your boy from time to time he will be able to apply for jobs in villages that are looking for an idiot, because we all yell. If yelling from time to time chipped away at baseline intelligence, then my own dear, sweet sons would be in a special school for children who used to be quite smart and are now barely able to speak. We all yell occasionally-ish; but if yelling is *all* you do, then your boy will pay for that.

And so will you, because when you are old he will put you in a really crappy old people's home where mean nurses will poke you with sticks. Fair enough. We should all remember that one day we will be old and feeble and they will be in charge. They will also, if we do a poor job, have access to sharp sticks.

11

Throwing like a girl: the gender similarities hypothesis

During the course of writing this book, I didn't travel to Wisconsin. I wouldn't want you thinking that I did, because I didn't.

Not even a little bit.

If I had, though, I would have gone to visit Professor Janet Shibley Hyde at the University of Wisconsin, because Professor Hyde is pretty much at Ground Zero when it comes to the debate about sex differences.

Remember, though, I've never met her. Never talked to her. Can't have because, like I said, I've never been to Wisconsin.

But if I had gone to visit her, which I haven't, then, in theory, it might have gone something like this . . .

A small nocturnal bird

On the day I never met Professor Janet Hyde, it was just starting to snow. I'd heard that Wisconsin winters are long and harsh, and the rapidly darkening skies seemed fairly keen to make good on that promise. The campus itself, nestled in over 900 acres of gently wooded, rolling hills beside the picturesque Lake Mendota, was every bit the American university. Even though the university has its fair share of high-tech glass-and-steel constructions, there were numerous old stone buildings that looked as if they'd been ripped straight from a film set.

I got to West Johnson Street without too much trouble, and before long found myself outside the Brogden Psychology Building at 1202, a fairly block-ish redd-ish stone building that seemed about what I'd expected a psychology building to look like. Somewhere above me on the fourth floor, hopefully, was Professor Hyde.

I paused briefly on the way into the building to disarm a mugger armed with a knife who was attempting to take an old lady's purse. Using techniques from the Israeli Krav Maga school of martial arts that I'd picked up from YouTube, I delivered a crushing knee to his groin, then locked his wrist, releasing the knife, and finishing off with a palm-heel strike to his nose.

'Why thank you, young man,' the old lady said.

'Don't thank me, ma'am – thank the good folks at YouTube,' I said, handing her the knife as a souvenir.

'You Australians are so brave,' she replied.

'I'm not an Australian, I'm a Kiwi.'

'A fruit?' she asked, looking suddenly confused.

'No, not the fruit. A kiwi is a small nocturnal bird from New Zealand, and that's also what we call ourselves: Kiwis.'

'Why would Australians name themselves after a small nocturnal bird from New Zealand?'

'They don't: I'm from New Zealand.'

She looked puzzled, and briefly I wondered how these people had ever become a global superpower.

In any case, about three minutes later – bang on time and slightly out of breath – I knocked on the door of room 410 in the psychology building, the very room that my old pal Google had told me was where I'd find Professor Janet Hyde.

'Come in,' a voice called from the other side. And I did.

The woman behind the desk looked every bit the college psychology professor. She was tall and slim, with wavy grey hair and an exceedingly warm smile. Her office was also very much the working space of an experienced academic. There were a few personal nick-nacks, a watercolour hanging on the wall and the inevitable piles of research papers in neatly appointed stacks.

'Can I help?' she enquired.

'Well,' I said. 'I'm writing this book about mothers and boys, and I'm wanting to show people how the "boy crisis" has been essentially manufactured by people who've got a particular political agenda. What's more, a lot of the stuff they use as evidence of some fundamental, innate difference between girls and boys is . . . well . . . a bit off.'

'Oh,' she said smiling. 'You're from Australia. G'day, mate.'

'Uh no, I'm a Kiwi.'

'You're a fruit?'

'No, not kiwi like the fruit, kiwi like the small bird. I'm from New Zealand.'

She simply looked confused. 'I don't quite understand.'

'Look,' I said, pushed for time, 'forget about all that. I'm particularly interested in your Gender Similarities Hypothesis. When I read that paper, it fair blew my socks off.'

'My paper?'

'Yeah,' I said, taking out a special gold pen I'd been given as a thank you by the airline for single-handedly thwarting a terrorist hijacking on the flight over, and a small notepad. 'You know the one?'

'I'm not sure I do,' she said.

Sighing, I realised that she was probably the absent-minded university professor type, so I started to explain. 'You remember the paper you published in 2005?'

She still looked blank. Fair enough, she must publish a lot of papers in her line of work, and I'm sure after a while they all blurred into one big clump.

'Let me recap,' I said, and began to remind her of the incredibly interesting research paper that had brought me all this way . . .

The Gender Similarities Hypothesis

Simply put, five years after the millennium Professor Hyde had been interested in what the complete picture of research on gender differences actually said. There has been quite a lot of it over the years, looking at all kinds of things, like abstract reasoning, mathematics ability, spatial perception, aggression, helping behaviour, sexual attitudes, throwing distance and cheating attitudes, to name but a few. At the outset, she formed a hypothesis that males and females were similar on most, but not all, psychological variables.

And why did she form a hypothesis before she'd even looked at anything, you ask?

Well the way science works is that you first form your hypothesis (or your theory) and then you go out and collect the evidence, analyse it and see if your original hypothesis was correct or whether it should be chucked on the pile along with other rubbish hypotheses like 'the Earth is flat', 'Elvis is still alive' and 'politicians really care about us'.

So once she had her hypothesis to test, Professor Hyde then went out and collected up all the best and most scientifically rigorous reviews she could find of the research that had been done so far. A review paper collects together all the published studies in a given area of interest and has a look at them to see if there are any common trends or findings. Effectively then, Professor Hyde produced a review of the reviews looking at 128 different abilities/attributes. She then subjected the findings about those 128 separate abilities to some statistical analysis to see if there were any areas in which males and females showed statistically significant differences.

You'd think, based on all the pop-psychology and pop-neuroscience books that have been written on this subject, that Mars and Venus would have very little in common. Which is why the results were, to put it mildly, quite surprising. Professor

Hyde found that 82% of the psychological variables that had been examined showed *no difference* between males and females. Out of the total of 109 variables that showed no difference, the following 23 variables are a small sample of some of the areas where males and females came out even:

◊ mathematics

◊ reading comprehension

◊ vocabulary

◊ science

◊ attributions of success and failure in tasks

◊ talkativeness (in children)

◊ facial expression processing

◊ negotiation outcomes

◊ helping behaviour

◊ leadership style

◊ neuroticism

◊ openness

◊ life satisfaction

◊ self-esteem

◊ happiness

◊ depression symptoms

◊ coping

◊ moral reasoning

◊ computer use

◊ job preference for challenge

◊ job preference for security

◊ job preference for earnings

◊ job preference for power

There were 11% of the psychological variables where there was a moderate difference between males and females, and these were as follows (greater effect size for males or females indicated in parentheses):

◇ spelling (females)

◇ language (females)

◇ mental rotation (males)

◇ spatial perception (males)

◇ smiling (females)

◇ smiling: aware of being observed (females)

◇ aggression: all types (males)

◇ physical aggression (males)

◇ verbal aggression (males)

◇ extroversion: assertiveness (males)

◇ body esteem (males)

◇ sprinting (males)

◇ activity level (males)

◇ computer self-efficacy (males)

A total of 5.5% of the psychological variables examined in the various reviews showed a large difference between males and females:

◇ mechanical reasoning (males)

◇ spatial visualisation (males)

◇ physical aggression (males), in some studies

◇ helping while being observed (males)

◇ masturbation (females . . . no, just kidding, it really was the males)

◇ attitudes to casual sex (males)

◇ agreeableness: tender-mindedness (females)

◇ grip strength (males)

And the very large differences between males and females?

Interestingly, when the hundreds of variables that psychologists and researchers had studied over the years were reviewed, statistically analysed and given a complete drilling, there were only two factors that emerged as having a very large difference between males and females:

◊ the speed an object is thrown (males)

◊ how far it is thrown (males)

So when we lay out all the various attributes and abilities that scientists have studied looking at the differences between males and females, and you think about all the books, and songs, and poems, and made-for-TV movies that have been written, and sung, and filmed, the biggest differences between us are how fast and how far we can throw a ball.

Edgy masturbation humour

I put down my special gold pen: 'See, that's the thing that got me, Prof: there really is such a thing as throwing like a girl.'

She frowned slightly: 'Well, yes, I suppose there is.'

'And isn't that the problem?' I continued. 'People start to look at scientific results and construe some ridiculous nonsense out of it?'

She nodded, and looked animated for the first time since I'd walked in and sat down. 'Yes, it's surprising how often scientific results get overinterpreted or even deliberately misinterpreted by people with a particular political agenda.'

'Why do you think that is?'

'Well, I suppose not many journalists actually understand the science these so-called experts are telling them about, so they simply report a story without any critical analysis.'

'I know,' I joined in enthusiastically. 'I mean, I could spin a whole thing on masturbation from your study.'

She frowned again and shifted uncomfortably in her chair. 'Pardon?'

'I could say that studies have shown that masturbation is the secret to male supremacy.'

'I *beg* your pardon?'

'Well, you've found that boys masturbate more than girls, and I could then theorise that this leads to better body esteem, better spatial abilities and more physical activity, thereby increasing health generally, increasing confidence with computers from accessing all that porn online, increasing grip strength and most of all the ability to throw balls faster and further because their arms are so strong from all the masturbating.'

She now looked distinctly alarmed. 'Why are you here, exactly, Mr ... ?'

'Latta,' I said, thinking that I'd clearly misjudged her sense of humour. 'Nigel Latta.' My instincts told me it was time to back-pedal. 'Clearly the big message in what you've found is that the best science we have so far shows quite conclusively that males and females are far more similar than they are different. That's not saying that males and females are identical, because they aren't. There are differences, and some of them are significant, but the reality is that we have far more attributes and abilities in common than are different.'

She frowned again, looking confused.

I pushed on: 'So what do you think the dangers are of over-stating the gender difference stuff? You know, that whole Mars and Venus thing, where we treat males and females as if they're from different planets.'

'I'm not sure what you mean,' she said.

For a smart woman she seemed a little vague about her own theory, which surprised me. I thought it only polite to help her fill in the gaps: 'Well, I'd think that one of the costs of the overinflated stereotypes is that we might believe that women really are more nurturing and men are always less nurturing. Imagine the impact of that on a new father if he's told that he can't be as nurturing as his partner. And for the women it's no better, because if they violate that stereotype, then they tend to get knocked back for it. Women leaders, for example, tend to suffer in their ratings if they violate the traditional norms of the nurturing female. Then, they tend to be seen as uncaring autocrats.'

'Well, that's not really my area,' she replied. 'But I suppose if you take the popular belief that boys are better at maths than girls, where does that leave the girl who has a natural ability in maths? Maybe her parents will have lower expectations of her? Maybe her teachers are less likely to see her natural ability and so she won't get the same encouragement a boy might get? And boys can get hurt by this as well. If boys get told they're not as good at reading, or they're not good at interpreting other people's feelings, then what effect might that have? If a parent thinks their son is not capable of being as emotionally empathetic as their daughter, they might lower their expectations of their son's ability to empathise with others. One can only wonder what the impact of that might be.'

I nodded sagely. 'You got that right, Prof Hyde.'

She frowned again. 'I'm sorry?'

'I said you got that right, Prof Hyde.'

'Prof *who*?'

'Hyde. You're Professor Janet Hyde, right?'

She shook her head. 'No, I'm Dr Leslie Graham, microbiologist'

'What are you doing in Professor Hyde's office?'

She frowned again. 'This is *my* office.'

'In the psychology building?'

She pointed out the window across the street. 'That's the psychology building.'

'Oh, bugger,' I said, taking out my carefully folded campus map. 'I don't understand how I got that wrong.'

'You should have asked someone for directions,' said Dr Graham.

'I didn't need to ask for directions. I have a map.'

'Yes, but if you'd just stopped and asked someone for directions, you wouldn't have got lost.'

'I'm not lost, I know where I am.'

'Only because I told you. If you get lost again, just ask someone for directions, OK?'

'I don't *need* to ask someone for directions, because I'm not lost. Besides, I have a *map*.'

Luckily just then a knock on the door made us both swivel in our chairs. A tall, burly man with dark glasses, a dark suit and a radio earpiece stood imposingly in the open doorway.

He looked so imposing, I guessed it was a skill he probably practised in the bathroom mirror at home.

'Mr Latta?' he said in clipped professional tones.

'Yes.'

'Mr *Nigel* Latta?'

'Yes, that's right.'

'I'm Special Agent Hanson, Secret Service. Mr Latta, the Secretary of Defence sent me. The President needs you.'

I sighed and looked at my watch: 12.10pm. That would leave me no time to go and talk with the real Professor Hyde, but, what the hell, I'd read her paper so it probably didn't matter all that much.

'Dr Graham,' I said, rising to my feet, 'You've been very helpful, but as you can see I'm needed elsewhere.'

'Of course,' she said, still frowning.

As I walked quickly down the corridor with Special Agent Hanson, he turned to me and said: 'By the way, my kids love that Crocodile Hunter guy on Animal Planet.'

I sighed. 'He's an Australian. I'm a Kiwi.'

'A what?'

'A kiwi, it's a small nocturnal bird . . .'

The moral of the gender similarities story

There is a *hugely* important message here for *all* parents raising boys, but for mums in particular, and it's this: he's more like you than he's not like you.

And why is that so important? It's important because it says that, in the great majority of areas, we are completely justified in expecting the same standards and levels of achievement from both our sons and our daughters.

They are more like you than they are different to you.

Now, I know what you're thinking: this seems completely counter-intuitive, because many mums think boys are a bit of a mystery. This is why the 'different-brain' proponents sell such vast numbers of books, because the stuff they're saying sounds more sensible. The 'different-brain' message appeals because, even though the research doesn't support many of the bold claims that are made, it just *feels* more right.

But, just for a moment, let's put our unsubstantiated feelings aside and review what the actual scientific evidence says just one more time. In Professor Hyde's well-respected and widely cited scientific review of the gender difference research, she found that there was *no significant difference* for 82% of the variables examined, and this included variables such as mathematics, reading, self-esteem, neuroticism and depression. There were moderate differences in 11% of the variables studied, large differences in 5.5% of the variables studied and a very large difference in only 1.5% of the variables.

Those results don't suggest to me that males and females are from different planets. If we were from different planets, I'd expect to see the numbers the other way round, with say 80–85% of the variables showing large differences, and 15–20% of the variables showing a very large difference.

Instead it's a paltry 1.5%, and even then that paltry 1.5% is how far and how fast we can throw balls.

What this all means is that if you have a group of individuals, and you want to separate them out into males and females, rather than testing their maths abilities, or their reading comprehension, or their self-esteem, or their leadership styles, or their ability to empathise, or anything else you can think of, your best bet is to ask them to throw a ball and then put the half that throws the ball the furthest in one group and call them boys, and the other lot in a group and call them girls. You will still get some boys wrongly placed in the girls' group, and some girls wrongly placed in the boys' group, but if you're going to try to sort out the girls and the boys based on some attribute, then throwing a ball is your best bet.

They are far more like you – at least in terms of their fundamental psychological abilities and attributes – than they are different to you.

'Yeah, yeah,' I hear you say. 'Well if we're all so bloody similar, then how come they *feel* so different, and why is it still so hard to understand them?'

Good questions. They do often feel different, and that's because they are.

So what's that all about, then?

Read on.

Part Three

Masculinity –
On the Nature of Boys

Many mothers feel like their sons are a different kind of creature altogether. They often feel they understand their daughters more, and their sons are a cause of complete bewilderment. I'm not sure it's actually true that mothers always do understand their daughters more, but I understand why they feel that way.

As we've seen, boys are not all that different to girls, at least in terms of their fundamental psychological abilities and attributes, which is all fine and well, but doesn't that just make it all the more confusing? If they're so bloody similar, why do they *feel* so different?

What are boys? What makes them tick?

In this section, I'm going to take you on a bit of a tour inside the minds of boys. What you always need to keep in mind as we're going along, though, is that this is simply my view, my version of the world of boys. Having said that, it's built on being one myself, raising a couple and working with a very large number of them, so I think that qualifies me to lead a guided tour like this.

But it can only ever be *my* view.

To truly understand your own boy(s), you will have to make your own way. There's nothing wrong with this, and nothing to be afraid of either. The greatest joy of being a parent is the act of discovery, the moment when some new feature comes into view through the far-off mists.

It is the great miracle of becoming.

So I can't tell you what you'll find on your journey, because none of us can know these things. What I can do is teach you how to navigate by the stars, and give you a compass for when the clouds come. That, some courage, sensible shoes and a packed lunch are all you'll ever need.

12

Man stuff:
masculinity in the new millennium

He is dirty, that much we can know. This archetypal boy has a natural affinity for dirt. Dirt does not scare him; instead it fascinates him, the clinging, concealing nature of it enthrals him. He never tires of seeing how much will stick.

At least one knee will be bloody, skinned on some road, or tree, or stony bank. A single plaster will hang from the bloody knee by one sticky arm, like a baby tooth waiting for some fairy to pluck it. He will be covered in scabs, and cuts, and bruises, because these things are simply the price that must be paid if you dare to tangle with the world.

Blood and mud are the tools of his trade.

He will be noisy, too. He will make noise enough to fill the world, to scare away the lions in the bushes, to make the giants tremble and hide. Noise is how he announces that he has arrived, and it is noise that helps him to find his brothers in arms. There is no quiet way with him, no natural hush. He wears silence like an older brother's scratchy woollen jersey on a hot summer day.

When he laughs, it consumes all of him. It starts in his belly and travels all the way from top to toe. Laughing is a serious business in his world, an act deserving attention and abandon in equal amounts. He will laugh at the silliest things because laughter is far too wonderful to waste on serious things.

His friends will be his kin, his henchmen, his loyal company. They will watch each other's backs, and rally to a comrade's aide. They will never leave a man behind, because that is not what men do. They stand together, and they fall together. That is the code that men live by, and this too is in their bones.

Passions will rule him; obsessions will drive his way. All boys are seekers of buried treasure; it is in their bones. He will collect stones and sticks and bugs and bottle-tops and all manner of trivia. He does this because he knows that these things are not trivial, that there is some deeper secret hidden among the stones and beetles and bottle-tops. So he scours the Earth for whatever new things have caught his eye, and he lines his pockets, and drawers, and shelves with the glittering treasures he finds.

He will spend as much time as he can bear gazing upon his treasures in quiet moments. At such times he will lift them up, and polish them, and re-arrange them in mystic patterns known only to the ancients. He knows that there are riddles contained in these supposedly trivial things, maps to even greater treasures.

His favourite place is somewhere far away from the grown-ups, some hitherto abandoned place. It might be high in a tree, or in some long-neglected shed. Perhaps a clearing among some trees, or a clay bank spattered with pine cones. He knows that his place is magic. It is the door to some whole other place. He knows that this is where adventures begin.

In his dreams he will lead great armies, climb great mountains, fight monsters beyond the reach of lesser men. He will commit himself to quests and missions and hopeless causes. He will fight against all odds, against raging rivers, against fierce winds and fiercer foes. He will take on the dark knight, and the evil tyrant king, and the dreadful soulless Baer wolves of long-forgotten times.

And he will win.

And when he returns home at the end of the day, exhausted from his crusades, worn by his travels and humbled by the courage of his friends, we can also know that when you ask him about his day, about what's been happening in his world, he will shrug his shoulders.

'Nothin' much,' he will say. 'When's dinner?'

I think there are components of the archetypal boy in all of us, including mums. To wildly varying degrees, we all hunger for adventure and danger and the longing to follow some greater cause, something bigger and better than we are, something that will both define us and outlast us.

Of course, the problem is that someone still has to buy the toilet paper when it runs out, and weed the garden, and give the cat its worming tablet. These things tend to seriously cut into our time for swashbuckling and mountain-climbing.

So how realistic is the archetypal boy? To be sure there are bits of the archetypal boy that live in all boys, which is why the description resonates. The bigger question, though, is what constitutes a *real* boy? What are they supposed to be like? This is particularly tricky for mums raising boys by themselves, because there is no real benchmark to go by. If you don't know how boys are supposed to be, then how do you know if your boy is heading in the right direction?

Maybe I'm missing something, but it's always seemed to me that debates about things like the nature of masculinity are the product of too much time and not enough to do. I don't see many CNN reports from refugee camps in Darfur where earnest journalists are standing around covering outbreaks of masculinity debates among the starving masses.

'Can you tell us what you can see now, Connie?'

'Well, at this time the situation is still fluid, but what I can tell you is that shortly after a UN aide convoy pulled into the main camp area a small group of men started to feel a little insecure and that quickly spread among the tightly grouped crowd and became a full-blown debate about the nature of masculinity.'

'Do we know anything about what's behind this outbreak, Connie?'

'Yes, Jeff. It seems that a small contingent of men in the camp have been experiencing a sense of disconnection from their traditional roles of providing for their families, and this has led to a mounting tension with feminist factions within the main body of the refugees.'

'And do we know if any Americans are involved at this point, Connie?'

'Well, as I said Jeff, the situation is still very fluid, but at this stage it doesn't look like any US citizens are involved in the debate that we know of.'

'Thank you, Connie. Keep us posted.'

'I will, Jeff.'

'That was CNN reporter Connie Bumblebee reporting live from the UN camp at Darfur, where details are just beginning to emerge about an outbreak of dissatisfaction with current definitions of masculinity. And now . . . let's return to the PGA where Tiger Woods has just . . .'

I rather suspect that in places like Darfur they're far more concerned with such things as trying not to starve to death. Fair enough, I say. We, on the other hand, have a lot more food, and a lot more time, so we tend to get a lot more wound up about this kind of stuff. We do what we always do with something that's pretty simple: we turn it into a bit of a fuss.

Now, I'm not even going to begin to get anywhere near the academic debate about masculinity, because it is such a quagmire it would take three books just to summarise it and even then all we'd have achieved is killing more trees. Honestly, you start reading that stuff and you get a headache after a while. I quite like trees and I don't like headaches, so I'm going to pretty much skip all that.

This is one of those areas that is so inherently and intractably political, you can't avoid being dragged into it, and you can't win, because no matter what you say someone is going to take some kind of issue with it. Either the feminists are going to think you're a sexist pig, or the masculinists are going to think you're a lapdog to the feminist agenda. Pig or dog? Not much of a choice, is it?

Essentially, after feminism swept in and changed the way the game was played, the guys then had to figure out what the heck they should do. By then men were starting to feel the pinch of all the advancements that women had made, and so they formed a movement of their own. One very vocal group across most of the Western world included divorced and separated fathers who felt they were being excluded from their children's lives. Having said that, a large part of the men's movement – although actually there was no one 'movement' as such, but all kinds of different groups – were middle-class men who weren't sure where they belonged anymore and were trying to figure that out.

We didn't have bras to burn, so many of us instead elected to band together in sweat lodges and perspire with other men in the fashion of the Native Americans. There was a lot of poetry, and beating on drums, and running about in the woods.

Like all movements, the men's movement contained some men who genuinely wanted to find a better way to be in a changing world, some men who just wanted to get away from their wives and hang out with guys, some men who didn't like women and wanted to blame the feminists for their own failings, and there were also probably some guys who just liked running about half-naked in the woods. I'm sure the feminist movement was much the same. In any group of people you tend to get the genuinely good-intentioned, the aimless, the axe-grinders and the crazies.

I'm not meaning to imply that the men's movement didn't have genuine concerns, because they did. One of the outcomes of feminism for men was that it did cause us to re-evaluate who we were. That was both inevitable and a good thing. The problem was that much of the early rhetoric was framed up along the lines of 'we are victims, too', which the feminist movement (who hadn't even been able to vote not all that long ago) quite reasonably had a bit of a problem with.

Actually, for a period of several weeks in the early '90s I joined a men's group myself. I was a student at that time, very politically correct, and incredibly earnest, and I thought that a men's group would be just the ticket to obtain a little enlightenment. I went along for a few weeks and at first it seemed OK. Guys would get together, talk about their shit, and it was all very groovy given that I was still only in my early 20s and had yet to learn that if you keep looking in your belly button you're just going to keep finding fluff.

After a while, though, it started to get a bit, well . . . without wishing to seem unkind . . . tedious. Guys would start talking about wanting to 'take back their power' from women and I'd start to get a little bored. I mean, is that like the feminists took your batteries out or something? I didn't know that I had 'power' in the sense that it was stuff women could take away from me. I found myself thinking a lot of Superman and kryptonite. Maybe it was the same kind of deal? Maybe the feminists were taking our kryptonite?

I stopped going after a few weeks. I'd like to say that it was because I'd reached some philosophical epiphany, but from memory it was because the group met on a night where there was something particularly good on telly. I can't remember what was on, just that it ultimately proved more interesting to me than sitting with a bunch of guys talking about power outages.

When I look around at the young men of today, it seems like they don't rate all that masculinity debate stuff very highly. It seems to me that they've moved on to other concerns. This makes sense given that they've grown up in a world where there are women prime ministers, women vice-presidential candidates and women CEOs. For sure, nowhere near as many as men; but they're there. Sexism still exists and probably always will exist, just as racism exists and probably always will exist, but new generations have seen game-changers. They've seen Margaret Thatchers, and Hilary Clintons, and Helen Clarks, and Oprah Winfreys. All these women changed the game, just as Barack Obama changed the game for African Americans on Tuesday, 4 November 2008.

And here's the thing for mums: I don't know that figuring out some essential definition of masculinity is all that important. Who cares what kind of man your boy is, so long as he's a good one? I'd imagine that if you're an Inuit guy, then the criteria for manliness are quite different to the criteria if you're a Manhattan guy. Similarly, a Mojave Native American guy might have different expectations of himself than a London guy. Even right here in tiny little New Zealand, if you live on the wild and windswept West Coast of the South Island you're going to be thinking a little differently to a public servant in Wellington.

The real issue then is probably not so much about figuring out some paint-by-numbers definition of masculinity, but trying to work out what some of the underlying principles might be that constitute being a good man.

So let's do that.

Personality:
everything changes, and
everything remains the same

One of the interesting things about people, both girls and boys, is that despite all the debate and the hoo-ha, we tend to end up being pretty much just bigger versions of what we started out as. It's long been my impression from talking to mums and dads about their boys that there are patterns that become evident from a very early age. Frequently, I will find myself nodding as a mum is describing her son, and thinking, *'Oh, right, he's one of those type of boys.'*

Here's a very common example of how that happens.

Kathryn is the mother of a somewhat challenging 10-year-old boy called Thomas. She came in because she was at the end of her tether and didn't know what to do anymore. Everything with this boy was a fuss apparently. I start off by getting her to describe the incident that had preceded her calling me.

'We were getting ready to go out,' she said, 'and I asked him if he was ready.'

'And what did he do?'

'He said that he needed to find his red socks.'

'His red socks?'

'Yes. He has this pair of red socks that he really likes, and he always wants to wear them. Except this time he couldn't find them, and because I was taking him to a movie I told him to hurry up. But it was like the more I told him to hurry up or we would be late, the more angry he got with me. And, I mean, it was *his* movie we were going to see.'

'So what happened next?'

'Well then he told me to shut up, and so I thought, right, I'm not putting up with any more of your crap and so I said we weren't going.'

'And then he melted down?'

She nodded, 'Oh, yes.'

I thought for a moment. 'Thomas is a pretty smart boy?'

She nodded.

'He spoke early, had a good vocabulary; people would think he was older than he is?'

She nodded.

'And he's always been very stubborn?'

A big nod.

'And is he very sensitive as well? To criticism, I mean.'

Nodding.

'So it's like he'll push and push and push you, and when you finally get angry and yell at him, he gets all upset and hurt?'

Nodding.

'He's exceptionally thin-skinned? Takes everything to heart, and when he's hurt he gets angry and lashes out?'

More nodding.

'Is the reason that he likes the red socks because he says they feel nice and smooth and his other ones are too scratchy?'

'Yes,' she said, much as one might when a palm-reader tells you that your uncle Jimmy had one leg when he actually did have one leg.

'And when he was just starting school, did he have a few

problems fitting in with the other boys? Maybe they all liked sport and he was happy looking for bugs at playtime?'

Now she frowned. 'Have you been stalking us?' she asked.

I laughed. 'No, I've just met Thomas quite a bit over the past couple of decades.'

So how was it possible for me to know so much about Thomas? Simple: he fitted a pattern I've seen a number of times over the years.

He was the archetypal stubborn boy. I've noticed in my very anecdotal way that archetypal stubborn boys share some fundamental attributes. They:

◊ are intelligent, usually not 'gifted' but often above-average

◊ tend to react angrily as a matter of course, and especially angrily if they feel hurt

◊ are hypersensitive to criticism and rejection

◊ are *very* thin-skinned and take everything to heart, because of this

◊ are usually very tactile, and like smooth, soft fabrics

◊ are very loving, empathic and thoughtful, when they're in a good mood

◊ are usually, oddly, very interested in bugs and dinosaurs, often way more than is usual for boys of that age

Now, I know that's not a very scientific observation, but there you go.

For me, the bigger question is not so much whether this is an accurate observation of one of the various types of boys out there – mostly because I'm completely convinced that it is an utterly accurate observation – but does this mean that these boys will always be this way? Will they forever be stubborn, or is change possible? And how best can we help our kids to drive the personalities they've got?

The 'Big Five' personality factors

In our life before children, my wife and I travelled to Africa, and it was one of the most amazing places I've ever been. We watched elephants landing in waves at a waterhole in Hwange Game Park like planes at Heathrow Airport. Obviously some baboon somewhere up in a tree was managing the whole process. I was actually charged by a large male baboon when I got a little too David Attenborough with a troop passing through the car park of our hotel. We also had breakfast with warthogs grazing round our table, and went prowling through long grass for rhinos with a trainee guide who was one of the most passionate naturalists I've ever met.

When I read in the guidebook that there was a good chance of encountering hippos, water buffalo and elephants on the path that led around the river from one of the hotels we were staying at, I was instantly mad keen to go off on our own exploring and get a little more Attenborough. My wife, who'd read the stuff in the guidebook about more people being killed by hippos, water buffalos and elephants than lions, took the view that this was a ridiculous thing to be doing. She won in the end, which is probably just as well, because we probably would have been variously trampled, gored and mauled to death if I'd got my rather reckless way.

Aside from the warnings about all the different things that could kill you, the guidebook also included a list of the 'Big Five': the animals that are considered very cool to see while you're there – lions, elephants, water buffalo, leopards and rhinos. Now, not wanting to be left out, psychologists have their own Big Five, except these aren't animals but personality traits, or more correctly personality superfactors.

I know, nowhere near as cool as the rhinos and the water buffalo – even with the superfactor bit – but there you go.

The thinking is that our personalities are composed of various combinations of these superfactors.

And why should you care?

Well, there's a really good reason why you should care, and something of great relevance to the business of raising fine young men as you are, but we'll get to that in just a moment. Let me just give you a brief rundown on what the Big Five are.

1 *Extroversion/positive emotionality.* This describes the tendency for a person to be actively and positively involved in their world. Extroverted people are bold, outgoing and energetic (ie, farters). At the other end of this superfactor, people are introverted, quiet, meek, inhibited and lethargic (ie, non-farters).

2 *Neuroticism/negative emotionality.* This superfactor relates to a person's susceptibility to experience negative feelings, to get distressed, and to feel anxious, vulnerable or guilt-prone. Basically, this one's all about how wound up you get over stuff.

3 *Conscientiousness/constraint.* This superfactor describes the tendency for people to vary in their ability to control their thoughts and their behaviours. People high on this superfactor are responsible, attentive, persistent and generally have their shit completely together. If you're low on this trait, you tend to be irresponsible, careless and distractible.

4 *Agreeableness.* This superfactor involves a whole cluster of traits that determine if you're nice to be around, or a bit of a pain. If you're high on this one, then you tend to be co-operative, considerate and empathetic. Low on this and you're more aggressive, rude, spiteful and manipulative.

5 *Openness to experience/intellect.* This one is the most debated of all the superfactors – mostly because researchers are still arguing over the small print for this one – but it essentially describes your tendency to be imaginative, and creative, as well as how quick to learn and insightful you are.

Using these five superfactors, or variations on them, researchers from around the world have studied how men and women, and boys and girls, are similar and different. It turns out that there are some personality differences between the sexes, and that these differences hold fairly well across a number of cultures. Men tend to be more assertive and take more risks, while women are generally more anxious than men and more tender-minded. So it seems that dads are more likely to let you jump out of the tree, and mums are more likely to worry about you breaking a leg. What's interesting is that these sex differences in personality can be detected in childhood and remain pretty constant across adulthood.

What's even more interesting is that these sex differences become less extreme as you go from prosperous and developed countries to less developed countries. It seems that the more equal access men and women have to education and the opportunity to thrive economically, the more different we become, at least in terms of personality traits.

As with all studies, though, the big thing to remember is that variation is the key. Saying that, on the basis of these types of studies, *all* men are more reckless and *all* women are more anxious is simply not true. Some men are more reckless, but then some women are pretty reckless, too, just as some men are real worry-warts. These are broad trends and, while they might seem to explain the general tendency of reckless sons seeing their mothers as 'just making a big fuss out of nothing', we always have to be careful when applying this stuff at the individual level, because sometimes it may not be neurosis but something far more useful.

If I had told my wife all those years ago in Africa, just as a for instance, that her reluctance to participate in my reckless do-it-yourself big-game safari along the banks of the Zambezi was simply an artefact of her gender's high score on the neuroticism/negative emotionality superfactor and had pushed on regardless, I may well have been trampled, gored and mauled to death by the other Big Five, the ones with teeth and claws. Sometimes it isn't being neurotic; sometimes it's just being sensible.

But the *really* interesting thing about all this personality stuff is when you start seeing if you can make predictions about where people will end up when they're adults based on how they are at age three, because it turns out you can. What's more, it also turns out that there are some really useful implications in these predictions for those of us raising boys.

So what do we know about personality change and development over the lifespan?

We now know that there are no discernible differences in the levels of personality development and change for males and females. So men's and women's personalities develop to the same degrees over the course of all our lives. We also know that personality traits remain remarkably stable over time, and in fact personalities remain much more stable throughout both childhood and adolescence than people had previously thought. Pretty surprising, huh?

Most of us would think that childhood and adolescence, in particular, are times of great change in personality. In fact, the greatest changes in personality occur in young adulthood. This seems to reflect the fact that young adulthood is the time when we finally have the freedom to be who we really are. Up until then, we are living under our parents' roofs and their rules. When we finally get out there into our own life, that's when we – and they – find out who we really are.

Personality traits continue to change and develop throughout adulthood and seem to peak sometime after age 50. The big message of hope here, particularly for mums struggling with sons of all ages, is that change is inevitable. He will continue to develop and change throughout the course of his life, just as you will. I always tell parents that so long as everyone is still breathing, there's hope, and it seems that the science is on my side. Change *is* always possible, right throughout the lifespan, and that is a vastly comforting thought.

Teach your boy how to drive his personality

In one of the longest-running and most successful longitudinal studies in the world, researchers from the University of Otago in New Zealand followed a group of over 900 children for 35 years. Among a huge pile of things, they found that there were five separate styles of behavioural presentations that were evident in the children at age three, and that these behavioural styles predicted how the children would be doing in many aspects of their lives 23 years later. From this, it's possible to get some ideas about how best you can help your boy (or your daughter, for that matter, although that's a different book obviously) to acquire the particular kinds of skills he's going to need in life.

As with anything, you always need to remember that these things are not written in stone or in discreet categories. I'm just saying that children who display these *general* characteristics *may* tend to get steered towards certain outcomes later in life. Don't overthink this one, because these are just some very general guidelines to help give you somewhere to start. It's a little like if you're just about to head out to sea, you first check the weather conditions to see what you might be up against. Once you know what the predictions for weather are, that can help guide what you take with you.

Undercontrolled

These boys tend to be irritable, impulsive, generally niggly and not persistent when it comes to completing tasks. Often they will only grudgingly have a go at something, make a passing grumpy attempt and then give up in a huff. This is kind of an Oscar the Grouch approach to life. The way that you can best help your boy not to grow into an Oscar the Grouch is to focus on the following skills and strategies.

◊ Help him learn how to relax and not get wound up by every little thing that goes wrong. Help him to understand that the world is an imperfect, inherently annoying place, and that once you accept that and stop fighting it, life is much easier.

◊ Give him lots of coaching in how to grow relationships with his friends. Encourage him to think about how his behaviour affects other people.

◊ If he has a tendency towards being negative, then teach him to be more flexible in how he interprets other people's responses to him. You can do this by simply asking him what else the other person might be thinking besides hating him.

◊ Teach him to manage his impulsiveness by rewarding self-control. Do things like putting a chocolate biscuit on a plate and telling him that if he can leave it there for an hour without touching it, he can have two biscuits. Or take him to a toy store and say that if he can walk through it without touching anything, he can choose something cool to do with you.

◊ Generally help him to relax, to not take things personally and to develop a flexible approach to thinking about problems.

Inhibited

As the name suggests, these boys tend to be shy, fearful and socially ill-at-ease. They prefer to follow rather than lead, and retire quietly to the background, watching rather than join in. This is the Snuffleupagus approach to life. For those of you who don't know, Mr Snuffleupagus was a large, brown, hairy elephant on *Sesame Street* who was so shy and retiring that the only person who could ever see him was Big Bird. He was a bloody big elephant, too, so that says something about how unassuming Mr Snuffleupagus really was. The best way you can help a Snuffleupagus is to focus on the following.

◊ Help him to practise being loud: he'll need help at first letting the world know he's there.

◊ Activities like music can be very helpful when kids are younger, because the shy boy can shine when he plays the piano or the drums. The music becomes his voice.

◊ Encourage him to do dangerous things. He needs to push himself to take risks and experiment with new things.

◊ Teach him that he will need to learn ways to speak up for what he wants, and to stand up to pushier people. His natural tendency will be towards being submissive, and so he needs to learn how to do the yin to that yang.

◊ Watch films like *Gandhi* with him to show him that sometimes the greatest changes don't always come from the people making the greatest noise. Sometimes it's the quiet ones who change the world.

◊ Generally he will need help to find his feet, and to push for what he wants. He needs to learn to stick up for himself and for the things that are important to him. He needs to see that, even though taking risks is hard, the payoffs are that his world gets bigger with each risk he takes.

Confident

These boys tend to be zealous and outgoing types. They are noisy, and brash, and full of their own beans. These boys don't need to formally announce that they have arrived, because their behaviour, demeanour and general volume do that quite nicely all by themselves. These boys are the 'Ernies' of Bert and Ernie fame. While there are lots of good things about these types of boys, there are still a couple of things that may help them steer a slightly less bumpy path through life.

◇ Again, a little impulse control will help these lads. They will have a natural tendency to follow whatever whim takes their fancy, which is fine, but this should sometimes be tempered with a little analysis. Teach your boy to stop and think before he leaps.

◇ Humility is a big one, instilling the basic understanding that he is not the centre of the universe and that we revolve around the sun, not the other way round.

◇ It also doesn't hurt to teach him that, while there are some amazingly powerful things that can come from being unconventional, that doesn't mean you always have to be 'out there'. Convention becomes conventional because a lot of people have done a thing a certain way and found that it worked. Sometimes following the crowd is the smart thing.

Reserved

Boys who would be described as 'reserved' tend to be apprehensive when asked to do something new. They aren't completely para-lysed with doubt, just, you know, reserved. These are more like the 'Berts' of Bert and Ernie fame. What this implies is a cautious approach to life, and a tendency to hang back a little for fear of getting it wrong. The following are some suggestions of ways you can help boys who have this kind of an approach to life.

◇ Teach him that mistakes are important, and that the only way you really learn something important is to get something wrong.

◇ You need to help him to turn around his associations with failing so that he sees the opportunity to screw up as a gift, not something to be afraid of.

◇ Also teach him that there are very few mistakes that will result in the actual end of the world (things like disco music, for example), and that most mistakes are survivable.

◇ Generally, just try to teach him not to take life so seriously, even the serious bits.

Well-adjusted

Not surprisingly, well-adjusted boys are well-adjusted. They tend to do things in an age-appropriate way without getting too wound up about anything. If something goes wrong, they deal with it and move on. They are fairly even in mood and behaviour. They're not perfect, but they're just pretty straight flyers. Again, there are some things you can do.

◇ Thank the gods for your good fortune. Light candles and sing songs. Whatever you do, don't do anything to anger the gods, tempt Fate or generally poke a stick in the eye of Fortune.

◇ Take all the credit for the well-adjustedness. Claim that your son's even temperament is all down to your parenting, even though in all honesty it probably has a lot more to do with genes than parenting.

◇ Give other people parenting advice, no matter how unfounded it might be in any actual experience of raising a more difficult child.

◇ Enjoy him, most of all enjoy him, because while all boys are fun, these types of boys are very low-maintenance fun.

Take-home messages

The personality factor stuff is interesting not only because it shows some fairly consistent gender differences across a number of countries, but also because it can guide you in helping your boy learn to drive his particular personality. We now know that personality attributes remain relatively stable across the lifespan, but at the same time continue to grow and develop. So if you think about personality as being like a car, we're all born with a particular model that is our own. While we can't trade cars, or buy him a new one, we can teach him to drive the one he's got more skilfully.

14

Values maketh the man

The God to whom little boys say their prayers
has a face very like their mother's.

JM Barrie, author of *Peter Pan*

It's pretty easy to see that if you start thinking about how your boy 'should be', then you can quickly get lost in a sea of scientific data, passionate opinions, philosophical ponderings and extended academic debate. So far, courtesy of the good Professor Hyde from Wisconsin, we've seen that, at least in terms of our basic abilities and attributes, men and women are more similar than we are different. While various studies have found gender differences, there are a far greater number of abilities and attributes that men and women share.

There are also some core personality traits that have shown fairly consistent differences between men and women, a finding that has also been replicated in a number of different countries around the world. Men tend to be more assertive and take more risks, while women tend to be more cautious and more tender-minded as well.

We've also seen – courtesy of my thwarted do-it-yourself safari on the banks of the Zambezi River in Africa – that having a tendency towards caution is sometimes a very good thing.

What's more, we've seen that very clever, articulate and sometimes irate people have been arguing about the nature of masculinity for a very long time. Many, many thousands of words have been written on this topic by people from right across the political spectrum. No clear answers have emerged from all this as yet, and probably none ever will. That, in my humble opinion, is what makes these kinds of debates so interesting, but at the same time often of little practical use. That's OK, though, because not everything should have a practical outcome: sometimes the process of debate is the outcome in and of itself.

On top of *all* this, and flowing as a constant background to *everything* you read in this book, and any other book on this subject for that matter, is the fact that *any* differences people talk about are differences between averages, which are sometimes relatively small, and often there is quite large variation between individuals.

For example, while the average score for 978 men tested on the completely fictitious Boomfarty Flatulence Audibility Factor (BFAF) scale might be a ripping 8.37 out of a possible 10, I might be a sneaky farter and score only a lowly 3.44 points on the BFAF. What matters most to me is not the average score of all blokes on the BFAF, but *my* score on the BFAF. It doesn't matter a jot to me that all the other blokes are farting away at 8.37 if I'm a sneaky wee soul way down at the 3.44 level.

So what then if you're a mum raising a son? How do you help your boy to be a good man if all the experts in all the universities, and think tanks, and communes, and government-funded committees, and shoe stores, and cafés and everywhere else that people meet together to argue about this stuff can't agree?

I think that the answer is that there is no answer. Is that a little frustrating? Probably, so let me explain a little more.

When I was a fresh-faced young psychologist working with families, I used to get really worried because I felt like I didn't know what the right thing to do was. I'd sit with families, and sometimes as they talked, and the situation became more and more fraught, I'd go into a wee panic because I didn't know if what I was thinking really was the answer. This went on for quite some time, but gradually I began to understand a fundamental point about life, and human beings, and how we all wind our way through the incredibly complicated business of being alive: there is no right answer. It doesn't exist. There is only what you do, and what comes after that.

I don't mean that you should just do any old thing because it doesn't matter. What I mean – and this is something I've learnt from both observing and being part of literally hundreds of thousands of decisions about families – is that you have to give up worrying about whether or not what you have done was the 'right' decision, because you will never know. You don't get to make the decision eight different ways and try them all out to see which one works out best. You can't wind the clock back and try again.

All you can do is make the best decision you can in the moment, based on as much *helpful* information as you can find, and by talking it through with whomever's about (even if it's just the little voice inside your head), weighing up the costs and benefits of each option, and then just going ahead and doing it. Then you see what happens, and deal with that.

Partly as a result of accepting that there is no magic answer, no paint-by-numbers approach to sorting stuff out, I have become increasingly drawn to the notion of principle-based approaches to help people figure out what to do. The reason for this is that principles are 'big picture' operators. I've talked about the fundamental principles that I believe underlie 'healthy' families in *Before Your Kids Drive You Crazy, Read This!*, and I've extended that out into the fundamental principles that I think apply to parenting teenagers in *Before Your Teenagers Drive You Crazy, Read This!*, and now I'd like to tell you about how I think principles can be helpful in trying to figure out how to grow boys into good men. First, though, to confuse things even more, and at the same time to paradoxically make it all a lot clearer, let me tell you the story of three boys.

Three boys

James, aged 15

James is a football nut. He needs football as much as, if not more than, he needs air. His boots are like a part of his body, and when he runs onto the pitch, he comes alive in a way that is striking. When he's on the pitch his concentration is absolute, and he gives it his all. This is the one time that a pretty girl will not distract him. Nothing will distract him.

He has only one focus, and that is to win.

That said, he is the consummate sportsman. He takes losing heavily, but he never takes it badly. He is the first to shake hands with members of the opposing team, and he does it with regret but not a trace of bitterness.

He's a popular boy who makes friends easily and well. He is loyal, and he'll go the extra mile for a mate who is in trouble. More than once he's stood by a friend who was getting picked on, and if asked he would say simply that that's what mates do for each other.

Girls love him. He's a good-looking boy and he has a certain trace of the pirate about him. He's a nice boy with just enough rough to give him a slight air of devil-may-care. He's had a few girlfriends, and his current one has been around for six months, which is a lifetime when you're 15. He likes her, but chicks are hard work so he's easy about where it all goes.

James's dad died when he was seven, and there isn't a day goes by where James doesn't miss him. When he was younger he used to cry, but not now. When the old pains come back, he takes his ball out to the back of the house and spends an hour kicking it into the wall as hard as he can. And most days that's enough.

He has no real ideas yet of where he's headed, but he does well enough in school to know that most things are an option for him if he wants. His big dream would be to play football for an English side, but he's never told anyone about that. When asked what he wants to do, he just shrugs his shoulders and says he's not sure.

He loves his mum, although he doesn't say it much these days. They fight a bit, mostly because he thinks she goes on too much about school, and dirty clothes left lying on bedroom floors, and dishes not put in the sink, and a thousand other things. No matter how bad things get between them, though, he never forgets that she's been there for him the whole way. She is the bedrock upon which his life has been built, and he never forgets that.

Not ever.

Steven, aged 10

Steven walks his own road, and has since the day he hit the ground. He's been hard work since the day he was born, and he's pushed his mother to the edge of breaking point, and occasionally beyond. He's not a bad boy, not by a long shot, but he's an incredibly stubborn boy. If there is a choice between the easy way or the hard way, he will choose the hard way every time. This tendency has made for some tough times, and more than a few tears.

Despite all this angry, stubborn, defiant posturing, he is a gentle soul. He notices things that other boys do not, and he is able to find the most delicate and intriguing ways to describe these things. He has always been a very articulate boy, and his stories have captured his teachers' attention all the way from preschool.

While he might be loud and obstinate at home, in the wider world he is a very quiet boy. His shyness is a constant hurdle that must be overcome. It is as if he feels the world that much more intensely than other children do. Just as he *feels* the beauty of a flower, he also feels the harshness of the world. The burden he has to carry is his sensitivity – to beauty, to the power of music to uplift, to the tactile delights of soft things, but also to harshness, and rejection, and aggression as well. All these things he sees and feels much more than other children.

He is also a constructor of magical places. The worlds he creates on paper, and with blocks, and in sand, and in boxes are reflections of the rich and varied landscape of his inner world. His mother sees the miracles he builds and senses that somewhere inside him are vast fields, deep jungles, walled cities and all manner of fantastical things, but he keeps all of this close. His inner landscape is a private place where only he is allowed to travel freely. The rest of us, if we're lucky, get a few postcards, but no more.

He could not be described as a popular boy, but he doesn't mind this. Somehow he just seems to understand that he isn't one of those boys. He doesn't like sport all that much, and he's never been one to run with the pack. He's not a pack animal. Having said that, he does have a smaller group of friends, all kids he's known for a long time, both boys and girls.

He has quite clear views about the future, and sees himself as a palaeontologist somewhere, digging up dinosaur bones and working away in a fossil-filled room in some university. His dreams are not conventional, but then what else would you expect from an unconventional boy?

He loves his parents dearly, although this is mixed in with generous helpings of wounded, stubborn grumpiness. Yet underneath this he is a very sweet boy, a boy who needs hugs, and cuddles, and all that stuff. Because this sensitive, intuitive boy understands the inherent fragility of the world, he needs to actually *feel* his parents' love, not just to be told about it.

He's a difficult boy to parent, but he's a wonder as well.

Jack, aged 7

Jack the lad is this one. He's a Tigger: he bounces. Jack finds it hard to be still, to be quiet. When he laughs, which is often, the world knows it. Often this will be to his teacher's annoyance and his own detriment, but he can't help it. A laugh has to be freed once created; there's no containing it.

He's rough is our Jack, and he'll often not notice that he's pushing things a little too far as some more delicate boy is upset at having been tackled to the ground. Jack notices but, because he gets caught up in the heat of the moment, usually only when it's too late, and even then he doesn't really understand because he thought it was all so much fun.

He's not the brightest boy in his class; in fact, he's about average, maybe a little below in some areas. He struggles with reading, and maths is a bit of a mystery to him. There's nothing he likes more than a good class project, though, because he loves to build things, anything is fine.

He gets in quite a bit of trouble at school. His nature isn't an easy fit with the modern schoolyard, and more often than not most weeks he'll have at least one stint sitting outside the staffroom at lunchtime for being too noisy, or too bouncy, or for some other infraction. Jack doesn't mind, though, he takes it with resigned good humour.

He has lots of friends at school, although only one or two good friends. Jack doesn't want intensity, he wants variety, and noise, and excitement, so flitting from one group to the next suits him just fine.

His favourite place in the world is his backyard with a hammer, some nails and some old planks of wood. The hammer is well-rusted from having been left outside countless times despite equally countless reminders, but it's well-loved just the same.

He forgets everything because he's so easily distracted – a fact that drives his long-suffering mother insane. She is raising Jack herself, because his dad left when he was only three. She worries about the effect this has on him, and feels bad that there are no good men in his life. She's looking, but they're hard to find.

Still, she knows enough to have bought him that hammer, and to not complain too much about the fact that her backyard constantly looks like a building site.

One of the remarkable things about Jack is that he has a strong sense of fairness and fair play. He won't let anyone be pushed around, and he will always go out of his way to help out if some other kid is in trouble. One of the reasons the teachers tolerate Jack's maddening bounciness is they've seen how, despite his tendency to push things too far, he always seems to notice if someone is in trouble in the playground, and more than once he's been the first one to let the duty teacher know that some younger child has hurt themselves.

He's a Tigger, he bounces, and it drives everyone mad – but he's a Tigger with a heart, and they're the best kind.

What makes a good man?

I think you'd agree that these are three very different boys. They have different interests and passions, and different approaches to life. They range from model student to difficult student, and their academic abilities vary as well. James is a popular boy; Steven is a bit of a solitary man in many ways; and Jack is, well, Jack's Jack. I think what's also quite clear from looking at these three boys is that chances are they're all going to grow up to be good men. James will probably be some kind of professional, married to a gorgeous girl who was probably very popular at school, but despite that will actually be a nice person. Steven probably will end up in some university somewhere with a girl who's complex, but fundamentally good. Jack might end up as a builder, or maybe a millionaire, possibly both. He'll be married to a good, sensible woman, they'll have some kids who will probably also have a bit of their dad's wild-boy in them, and he'll coach their sports teams. In any case, I'd predict they're all going to grow up to be good men.

Now, if you tried to figure out how to make a James, a Steven or a Jack, it would be impossible. A lot of it is probably genetics, with a fair helping of environment as well. They all have elements of the archetypal boy, but they are all unique variations on the central theme. What is clear, though, if you look at these three boys, is that while the content of who they are may vary, they seem to share some fundamental values between them. The surface details may vary a lot, but underneath them are some overarching principles that seem to guide the decisions each boy makes.

The various incarnations of the 'good man' are all around us to see, and they are many and varied. Gandhi was clearly a good man, as was Oskar Schindler, Paul Newman and Martin Luther King, Jr. All complex men, some more flawed than others, but all inherently good men who did good things with their lives. Even contemporary figures like the incomparable Bear Grylls of *Man vs Wild* fame. This ex-military special forces, mountain-climbing, bug-eating, adventure-loving man is also a good example of the modern good man. He's rugged, but isn't all macho, and can get very sensitive when looking at a panorama in the Sahara or a Sumatran jungle. Despite this, he was a member of the elite British SAS (which, for the benefit of all the mums who don't know, is the Special Air Service, now part of the British Army's Special Forces group) and could probably kill you in six different ways. He probably *has* killed people when he was in the army, but I'd imagine he's a great dad to his three little boys, and he's a bloody good example for all the other boys who watch him. My boys certainly love watching Bear eat bugs, kill and skin monitor lizards and jump into quicksand. It's fantastic boy stuff from a bloke who I'd wager is actually a very nice man to boot.

The faces of masculinity are many and varied, which is why I think that the most important thing for mums to understand about how to raise a boy who will eventually become a good man is that it isn't really about teaching him how to be 'masculine' or how to do 'man stuff', because with a little bit of guidance and a little freedom to run wild he'll find out these things for himself. In fact that's the only way you can find out what 'man stuff' is when you're a little boy: it's to go out and try it. Instead what I think you need to do, your piece of this particular journey, is to focus on teaching him *values*.

This might seem a little old-fashioned, and I certainly wouldn't want to give you the impression that this book has some secret right-wing agenda. It doesn't. You won't find me out marching with big signs telling other people that they're going to Hell because they don't have the right-shaped 'family values'. Actually, one of the funniest things I've seen in a long time was when a reporter asked a demonstrator – who was in the middle of marching down a road with hundreds of other similarly zealous types all chanting some slogan or other about 'family values' – just what his favourite 'family value' was. The guy paused, and looked a bit stumped. It went something like this:

'What are you out here protesting about today?'

'We're out here marching for family values.'

'And why is that?'

'We think that politicians have lost their way. Everywhere you look, family values are being eroded and the ones who are going to pay for that are our children.'

'So, what's your *favourite* family value?'

A slightly taken-aback, flummoxed kind of pause: 'Pardon?'

'I just wondered what your favourite family value was?'

Another longer pause. 'Ummm . . .'

The reporter left the microphone hanging there for ages as this guy desperately tried to think of something to say. Nothing came. It was very, very funny.

So I'm not part of that 'family values' set by any means;

instead, I'm talking about values in a very pragmatic sense. It's always been my view that we call values 'values' because they are principles or ways of being that we actually *value*. They are like an inner code of conduct that's important to us. They are the rules we operate by. Our values form the cornerstones of who we are, and have a massive impact on what we do, and where we end up in life. For example, if one of your core values is excitement, then you are far more likely to end up on top of a mountain than someone whose core value is security.

It's my belief that our values are inherently wrapped up in both our biology and our environment. Personality and temperament are major driving forces in determining our values, just as is our environment. If you grow up in an environment in which the predominant values are selfishness and a me-first attitude, then you are likely to pick up quite a bit of that in your own life. Our prisons are filled with boys who grew up in homes where they were taught these kinds of values. They internalised those messages and carried them out into the world. They were taught values – just the wrong kind. I've spent many, many hours sitting with men where the greatest tragedy is that you can see the ghost of the man who could have been if only someone had helped him find his feet.

So in my humble and somewhat-informed opinion, what you should do is teach your boy the kinds of core values that will help him to be the best man that he can be in the world. If you can manage that, then you'll have done your job.

Core values

Responsibility, Humbleness, Compassion

There are likely to be many views on what are the most important core values to teach boys. This is the kind of stuff that researchers and philosophers can spend their whole careers arguing about.

I've thought about this one for a long time myself, and whittled the list down to three core values that I think pretty much encompass the bigger picture. Remember, these are just what I think based on all the stuff I've seen. You may well have your own ideas, and in fact I hope you do. There is no 'one true way' with this stuff, because it isn't that kind of deal. These are just my thoughts, which you may want to use as a starting point from which to organise your own thinking about core values.

Responsibility

Fundamentally, this is about responsibility for self and for your actions. This means instilling in your boy a sense that *he* is responsible for his own life – no one else. As the saying goes: it isn't what happens to you that defines who you are, it's how you respond. The world owes none of us a living, and none of us are inherently special in the eyes of the world. The world doesn't even know we exist, and so it is up to each of us individually to find our own way.

Everything you do, even if it is just a thought, has some kind of consequence out there in the world. In Eastern philosophies this is called karma, or dependent arising. In Western science it is called Chaos Theory (which is the mathematical theory that small initial differences can have a great impact further on down the line – the idea that a butterfly flaps its wings in Turkey and that sets in motion a chain of events that results in a tornado in Tokyo). Whatever you call it, and however you think of it, everything you do has a consequence, and understanding that is important.

Too many young men act as if the complete opposite is true. They seem to think that nothing will hurt them, and if anything bad happens then it isn't their fault. Some of this is because their parents step in far too much and take ownership of their sons' problems. If he gets in trouble, they dig him out. If he screws up, they fix it up. This is *not* how you teach children responsibility.

The way you teach responsibility is to make them responsible. If they make a mistake, then they fix that mistake up. If they do wrong, then we make them find a way to make it right again. This doesn't mean that you abandon them, or that you don't support them; in fact, it's completely the opposite. You support them in whatever way you can to face the consequences of their actions. It is only through facing the consequences of their actions, through understanding at a very deep level that they are responsible for the outcomes of their actions, that they will learn to think carefully about where they place their feet.

Humbleness

To practise humbleness is to understand that we are part of the world, not the centre of the world. Humbleness does not mean that you need to be meek, or quiet, or submissive. Humbleness is about understanding that we are all part of something much bigger than any one person. Humbleness is about adopting a sense of perspective about our place and purpose in the grand scheme of things. None of us got where we are by ourselves; we all stand on the shoulders of those who went before us.

I also think an integral component of humbleness is respect for others. Again, this does not mean always surrendering your needs to other people's needs, or always acting as if everybody else is right and you're wrong. Instead, I think this facet of humbleness is about having basic respect for others, for your parents, your teachers, the police and all the other people with whom you come in contact.

Again, we model this by not going off our nut at the hapless bank teller who happens to be the only one on duty, meaning that the queue is long and arduous. Respect is about expressing what you're not happy about in a way that acknowledges that the other person matters and has feelings.

Compassion

This one really speaks for itself, but at its heart is the fundamental notion of caring for others. Without this, we are somehow less than human. Of course there are very few people in the world who are completely without compassion, but there are many people who seem to put compassion pretty low on their list of values. One doesn't have to be especially mean for this to happen; it can be as simple as a lack of action. It can be the act of seeing something bad and turning away from it. Fundamentally, the way that compassion works in action is to understand that we should look after the little guy. It is as clear and as simple as that.

Look after the little guy.

Teaching values

How then, does one go about teaching values to a growing boy? One of the easiest ways to get your head round this is to think about values as being like a compass. The purpose of having values is so that when the fog rolls in and it is hard to know which way to go, your compass can always point to true North. Even when you are completely lost, you will always know which direction you should follow. You might not be able to see very far ahead into the swirling mists, but at least you know you are headed in the right direction.

So then the question becomes: how do you teach a boy to read a compass?

Step 1: Model it by using a compass yourself on a daily basis

The first thing is to convince him that the compass is actually useful and to show him that it can help. In the first instance, the way that he can see that is by watching you use your own compass. It is in seeing how you enact your own values that he will first begin to learn about how to conduct himself. You cannot tell him to take responsibility for his actions if you aren't taking responsibility for yours.

James and his mum are in a queue at an automated machine that validates parking tickets. There is an older woman at the front of the queue who is clearly flummoxed by the machine. She doesn't know where to insert the ticket and keeps putting it in the wrong slot. There are several other people in the queue who are starting to get impatient and frustrated, which only adds to the poor woman's pressure. James's mum leaves her place in the queue, walks to the front of the line and asks the woman if she can help. The offer is gratefully accepted, and she helps the woman to validate her ticket and then explains which way it goes in the machine at the exit. The woman thanks her and moves off, thus freeing up the queue again. James's mum doesn't say anything to him. She doesn't need to. Her actions told him more than a thousand lectures ever could.

None of us is perfect, however, and we all stray daily from the road, but we should try as hard as we can to model the values we want our boys to adopt for themselves. It is also all right to talk to them about how hard it is sometimes, about how difficult it can be sometimes in a busy jam-packed life to follow one's values.

We all get grumpy, and we all overreact sometimes. There is nothing inherently wrong with this; it's just the price you pay for being less than a saint.

What is important, though, is to acknowledge when you have dumped your bad day on them. Dumping your bad day on them is not modelling responsibility – *apologising* for doing it is. If they see you actively navigating by reading your own compass, then it will be easier to convince them that it really can be helpful to find your way when you're lost.

Step 2: Explain how a compass works

The next step, once they've seen the benefits of using a compass, is to explain how it works. An *actual* compass works by suspending a small piece of metal (the needle) on an almost frictionless point, thus allowing the metal to align itself with the Earth's magnetic current. If you imagine a magnet running from the North Pole to the South Pole, then all the needle is doing is lining itself up with the magnetic field that runs roughly from North to South. So the needle doesn't need to see where it is going, it simply follows this very weak electromagnetic field that runs through the Earth. The needle aligns itself with an unseen but very real force that can be found everywhere from Iceland to the Sahara.

Values are analogous to the needle, because values align themselves to some greater truth, a weak but very real force that can also be found everywhere from Iceland to the Sahara. If you are lost in a blizzard – or in a sandstorm, for that matter – your compass will always tell you where North is. Similarly, whether you are lost in a blizzard or a sandstorm, values such as responsibility, humbleness and compassion will help to inform your actions. If you are lost in a sandstorm and understand that you are ultimately responsible for your choices, and also have a sense of humbleness in the face of Mother Nature's fury, then you are more likely to make better decisions.

Of course if you had watched Bear Grylls on *Man vs Wild* you would also know that the best thing to do in a sandstorm is to find a dead camel, gut it and then crawl inside the camel's body. This of course requires a knife, a dead camel and a tolerance for dark, enclosed, stinky spaces.

Step 3: Let the boy practise

Ultimately, the only way to learn how to use a compass is to actually get out there and have a go. There is no greater sense of achievement than the sense of having mastered some important skill, and compass-reading is one of life's most important skills in my opinion. Sometimes this will mean that your boy might get lost, or end up stuck in a bog because he went the wrong way. There's nothing inherently wrong with screwing up, and I'd pretty much be of the view that if your boy isn't screwing up from time to time then he's probably being far too cautious. Screwing up is how we learn important lessons, and it's a fair bet that if you take a wrong turn and end up stuck in some swamp, then you're going to pay more attention next time to where you're heading.

Jack and his mum are talking one night at the end of a particularly difficult day. His mum got called in to school because Jack got in a fight with another boy in his class.

'So what happened?' his mum asks.

Jack shrugs with shoulders that seem to have been struck glum.

'Who started the fight?'

He shrugs again.

'Did he hit you first or did you hit him?'

'I hit him.'

'How come?'

Shrugs again.

'C'mon, Jack. It isn't like you to get into a fight. What happened?'

'He was saying mean stuff to me.'

'Like what?'

'He was saying that I'm dumb because I'm not in the top reading group.'

'Oh, yeah, that's pretty mean. So why did you hit him?'

'Because he was mean.'

'So you hit him?'

'Yeah.'

'Did it help make you feel better?'

Shrugs.

> 'So, how did you feel?'
>
> 'I dunno. Bad, I guess.'
>
> 'Do you think he's right? Do you think you're dumb?'
>
> Shrugs.
>
> 'If I said to you that you should always listen to mean people because they always tell the truth, would you think that was a smart thing to say or a dumb thing to say?'
>
> 'Dumb.'
>
> 'See: you're a smart guy. When people are being mean they aren't saying anything that's true, they're just trying to make you feel bad to make themselves feel better.'
>
> 'I guess.'
>
> 'If that kid is being mean because he feels bad, should you hit him or should you try and figure out a way to help him feel better?'
>
> 'I guess I should help him feel better.'
>
> 'Smart boy.'
>
> 'Mum?'
>
> 'What?'
>
> 'Can I have some ice cream?'
>
> 'Nice try, Jack. No.'

Debriefing afterwards is usually the best way to help your boy figure out where he went wrong. The idea is not to lecture or to wag a finger, but to adopt an attitude of genuine curiosity, of co-operative problem-solving. If you're met with grumpiness, then you can always just ask a question and leave it hanging. Something like: 'I wonder what else you could have done here? Still, I don't have to go on about that, because I know you're a smart-enough guy to work that one out all by yourself.' The beauty of questions is that you don't have to have it answered out loud. Just the act of asking a question is often enough to start the conversation, even if the whole conversation is entirely private and happens inside his head.

Part # Four

Raising Boys
in the Real World

So now we've set the context for what comes next, which is of course a tour through some of the nitty-gritty stuff about actually raising a boy. My intention here is to cover off the big issues, the major things that cause mums grief, the meat and potatoes of growing boys.

15

Communication: the language of boys

There is no greater joy than truly communicating on a deep level with another human being. Of course, the swing side of that is that there's nothing quite as frustrating as not quite communicating either.

You'd think, on the basis of all that science saying men and women aren't all that different, that we'd be pretty good at communicating with each other, but unfortunately that doesn't seem to be the case.

Anyone who says that men and women talk about things the same way would be a mug. While it might be true that men and women use about the same number of words in a day, we do seem to use them in different ways.

Of course, this isn't true across the board, because there are lots of times when you could take a transcript of a conversation and you wouldn't know whether it was a man, a woman or a transgender train driver saying the words. I'd imagine that a female CEO talks in pretty much the same way as a male CEO, as do doctors, dentists and mechanics; but it's in our relationships with our loved ones that it all seems to get a little tricky.

There seems to be a tendency towards misunderstandings and misconstrued meanings and misplaced assumptions to the extent that often, even though everybody is saying the same thing, we all end up arguing on some fundamental issue like we were the bitterest of foes. Sometimes we end up battling as if our lives depended on it, when really we're talking about picking up the bathmat.

On top of all that, the ability to communicate effectively is an increasingly valuable commodity in this hyper-connected e-world of ours.

Sometimes just having the idea is enough to get you there, but often the communication of that idea is just as important. In fact, sometimes you can come up with a pretty crap idea, but if you can find a convincing way to sell it then people will flock to you. How else would you explain the exorbitant prices some people are willing to pay for 'designer' bottled water?

'Look, I've got this great idea.'

'What?'

'We're going to take water, put it in fancy bottles and charge people huge amounts for it.'

'For water?'

'Yeah.'

'And all you're going to do is put it in fancy bottles?'

'Yeah.'

'It'll never work.'

But, of course, it does, and the reason it works is because people are willing to pay a lot of money to drink something that they've been told you have to be special just to own.

I drink, therefore I am, the marketers told us, and some of us were so gullible, and had enough disposable income, that we actually believed it.

So how do you teach your boys to be good communicators? Well, I've got a few suggestions about how to do that, but first there are some general principles of boy talk that you need to understand, because they apply to all stages of boydom from the littlest to the biggest.

Pragmatism

One of the driving forces of boy talk is pragmatism. There isn't a lot of fluff in boy talk, not much padding. Boys tend to go straight for the heart of the matter without too much warm-up. Sometimes that can come out a little rudely:

'Why does Aunty Jane's house smell funny?'

'This tastes gross.'

'Don't kiss me at school, that's dumb.'

'Give me the butter.'

It isn't the boy's intention to be rude per se in these examples – despite the fact that all of these examples technically *are* rude – but rather it's just about getting what needs to be said said as quickly as possible. Why waste five words when three will do?

What you need to do with boys is always connect up the benefit to them of communicating in a particular way. Manners are a good example. We all want our kids to have good manners, and mums particularly so, because mums generally feel like they'll get the blame for mannerless children. The way you teach boys to use manners is to keep hammering home the message that manners are a tool, manners are useful because they help to create a good impression and good impressions mean you get invited back. At home, manners are useful because they will get you the thing that you're after and avoid the punishments that a lack of manners will always incur.

If he understands the concrete gains he can make by communicating more effectively, then he's more likely to do it. Girls are more likely to do something just because it's 'nice' to do it, but boys need to know what they get out of it. This doesn't mean that they're inherently selfish; it just means that as a general rule boys need to see the reason for doing something.

As he gets older, this becomes even more pronounced. The teenage boy is the arch pragmatist, and for many boys of this age they will use the bare minimum of words necessary for human survival. They don't see the point of telling you about their day, because it's already happened. What's the point of talking about it? Besides, most teenage boys will tell you that if you answer one of your mum's questions, it will immediately be followed with several more. Better just to shrug and mutter, 'I dunno.'

Less is more

This section is a little hard to write without sounding like a patronising, misogynist throwback to the '50s, but it needs to be said just the same. I'm also writing this section bearing in mind the study by Dr Matthias Mehl, from the University of Arizona, which showed that males and females tended to use on average about the same total amount of words per day. I don't doubt this, and yet still I feel compelled to write this section. You see, it has been my observation over all these years that mums tend to use a lot more words than dads when they're talking to their children, and specifically when they're telling them off. Mums tend to . . . well . . . you know . . . *go on* about stuff a bit much.

There, I said it.

I'm not sure if anyone's done any research looking at how mums and dads tell kids off, and more specifically how they talk when they tell kids off. I had a pretty good look, but I couldn't find any. If you know of any, please email me and tell me about it because I'd love to see it. In the absence of any hard scientific data, let me just share with you the insights gained from the better part of two decades working with boys and their mums and dads.

The problem is that mums, as a general rule, often think that the total number of words used is equal to the effectiveness of the message itself. There is a maternal tendency to embellish a simple instruction with a number of qualifiers, and modifiers, and certifiers, and sometimes blurtifiers, to such an extent that the original message can be completely lost.

The truth is that the more words you use, the less effective your message becomes. The more you say, the more opportunity you give him to argue with you. You cannot talk him into reasonableness, because he's an arch pragmatist and so he won't change for words – he'll change when there is a good reason to change.

Stop talking, start doing.

My humble suggestion for when you're asking your boys to do something, or telling them off for having done something wrong, is to use as *few* words as you possibly can. This will almost certainly be fewer than you're using now. If you keep the words to a bare minimum, you also keep the arguments to a bare minimum.

Anger is how he says most things

Boys feel just as many emotions as girls, and are no less complex emotionally, they just don't spend as much time talking about all that stuff, and they don't show anywhere near as much of it. It's been my experience that boys tend to express most of their unhappiness, stress, dissatisfaction and general malaise with anger.

Why?

I think it's because many of the messages boys get about their feelings are of the 'tough it out' variety. While there are all kinds of different masculinities out there, the strong, silent type is clearly one of them. It comes from everywhere and nowhere as well. I certainly don't think it's mums giving boys these messages; instead, it comes from television, storybooks, computer games, friends . . . all kinds of places. There's nothing wrong with strong, silent types per se, and toughing it out is often a useful approach when things get difficult, just so long as you have the option of being a little less silent and a little less strong if you need to.

I'm not going to get all whiney about poor boys being picked on by popular culture, or throw out that trite old line that masculinity has been demonised in an increasingly feminised world, because that simply isn't true. If you look at how men are portrayed on television and in films, we come across pretty well. Boys tend to save the day more than girls do.

Which just goes to show how easy it is to get pulled off into a completely unproductive discussion about the social construction of masculinity.

For our purposes here in the real world, all that matters is that you understand that anger is how boys express many of their negative feelings, that it's quite normal and that you can help him by teaching him how to express some of that other stuff in different ways.

Talking crap is good

There is an awful lot of banter in boy talk, and much of it is pretty inane. My wife can talk on the phone to one of her friends for half an hour and they actually talk about real stuff. I can spend the same amount of time on the phone and cover off issues like my latest idea to start albatross-wrestling tours, which then moves on to discussing my friend's suggestion that instead we put harnesses underneath them and we hang-glide with them and we end up by compromising and deciding that first we'll hang-glide off them, and then wrestle them when we land because they'll be more tired.

Boys can have serious conversations, but we far prefer to talk crap. It's just a lot more fun.

Your son will enjoy talking inane crap with you as well. In fact, one of the great joys of boy talk is that you can have these little bursts of conversational flimflam. This is where telling your boys (especially little guys) outrageous lies will make them shriek with laughter, and think you're very cool indeed. Lying to boys is crucially important and one of the best things about being a parent. Dads often grasp this fact instinctively; mums need to work it around in their heads a little. Take as an example this question from an eight-year-old: 'What was your school like?'

You could answer it with any of the following:

a) It was good fun. We had much smaller classes, but my teachers were very nice and I enjoyed maths and reading most of all.

b) I never went to school. When I was very little, I ran away from home to join the circus and spent 10 years as Matilda the Great Tightrope Hopper. Other people walked the tightrope; I hopped.

c) My school was run by a troop of very wise monkeys who taught us everything they knew about fruit.

d) I was eaten by a shark on my way to school when I was five, so I never learnt to read or write.

e) Our school was stolen by a herd of angry cows, so we had to sit in trees and write with sticks on the bark.

f) Some other crazy thing you make up . . .

Answer (a) is all right, I suppose. It's honest and communicates some real information . . . but (b)–(f) are a lot more fun.

Giving each other shit

I think it would be fair to say that one of the things mums find the hardest to understand about the way boys (and men) communicate is the way they constantly give each other shit. Now, I'm sure there are any number of political types who would see this as a toxic part of masculinity, and talk about how this enshrines outmoded macho stereotypes and all the rest of the blah-de-blah. In truth: it's just good fun.

Take for example this conversation between two six-year-old boys facing off with light sabres:

'You're a fart.'

'You're a bigger fart.'

'You're such a big fart that your pants fall off.'

'You're such a big fart that you can't even wear pants.'

'Yeah? Well you're a fart with pee in it.'

At which point both boys collapse on the floor in genuine delight at their articulate summing up of the other's character.

Now, some mums might be alarmed at this conversation. They might feel the need to intercede and instruct these two fine, flatulent young men that friends don't talk to each other like that.

'Friends should say nice things to each other,' that mother might say.

Actually in the world of boys, *real* friends call each other big farts.

Words, meanings and feelings

Words are interesting things, because they aren't just simply neutral collections of letters. They come with baggage. For example, you can describe visiting your in-laws in the following ways:

a) challenging

b) interesting

c) fun

d) penance

e) soul-destroying

All of which create a very different picture of what Sunday dinner at the in-laws' is like. It's the same with our children, because the words we use to describe the experience actually go a long way to create the experience. What we now know is that when we physically experience an emotion such as anger or fear, there isn't a lot of physiological difference between the states. You can't hook someone up to a machine and measure anger as a distinctly different physical response to fear, because your heart beats pretty much the same way in either state. The process seems to be that something happens to us, we experience physical arousal and then we make a decision about what those physical feelings mean – say, for example, 'fear' or 'anger' – and that then becomes the emotional experience:

physical arousal + decision about meaning = emotion

All this is intensely relevant to us as parents, because obviously the second part of the equation is something we can have some influence on. If we can give our children more options when it comes to making decisions, they may well end up with a much more flexible and adaptable emotional life.

The boy-ology of communication

In this section I'm going to give you my top three communication tips for each size of guy, from the littlest guys all the way through to big guys. I decided on three because – quite apart from the general spookiness of things that come in threes that we talked about at the beginning of Chapter 1 – three is all you need. There's no point in giving you 20 because you won't remember them. So three is enough. Three will do just nicely.

Little Guys

(2–6 years)

Recall from our discussion way back in Chapter 1 that Little Guys are pretty cool. They just are. When it comes to communication this is also a really important stage, because this is where they are first starting to put words together to help them understand the world, and to interact with it, and, as we've just seen above, if you learn a whole bunch of words to interpret and understand your feelings, you're going to be able to respond more flexibly than someone with fewer words.

Little Guys are great because they often seem to feel a fairly narrow range of emotions, but they experience them with an intensity that is, quite frankly, bloody amusing sometimes. Anger is a big one, and it peaks around two to three years old. This is when the tantrums first appear. Your precious little 18-month-old suddenly tips over into rages of major proportions but thankfully very small-scale. There will often be screaming, and drumming of little feet on floors, and throwing of things, and general rage.

If you ever think that your guy is over-the-top, go on YouTube and type in 'tantrum'. They *all* go completely mental at this stage.

It's like a little wave of fury sweeps over their developing brains and they simply can't stop it. They have to wait until it burns itself out. At this point the tantrums are mostly brought on by frustration that they can't do something they want to because you won't let them, or they simply don't have the fine motor skills to actually do it, or they can't have the red cup. (Usually there's a red cup in there somewhere. If it isn't red, it'll be something like red.)

I am also constantly amazed at the ease with which Little Guys' hearts break. Little-Guy hearts are incredibly fragile, and anything from being put in time out to not being able to watch Spongebob on television can smash them into a thousand pieces. Fortunately they can mend themselves in seconds as well, so that takes some of the pressure off.

My top three communication tips for Little Guys are as follows.

1 *Have fun.* This is just such a great age that you need to make the most of it. Have as many silly conversations as you possibly can. Wonder about butterflies, and the nature of puddles, and building blocks. Talk as much as you can stand.

2 *Give him lots of options.* If he knows that as well as being angry there is also happy, sad, confused, scared, surprised, brave, gloomy, melancholy (Little Guys love that word), lugubrious, joyful and all the rest, then you'll be instilling in him from the very beginning that there are options aside from just being angry or happy. If you ask your Little Guy if he's feeling 'gloomy', and make sure you say it in an over-the-top funny way, he'll love it, even if he *is* feeling gloomy.

3 *Lie to him outrageously and often.* I cannot stress enough the importance of telling lies to Little Guys. It is tremendous fun – for you and him. This is the age where they'll believe any old nonsense you tell them, and so you have the power to create a world of magic and wonder around them. This is a colossal power, but it doesn't last long, so use it while you've got it.

Life is a serious business, but in my humble opinion it's important to start teaching them from a very early age that, just because it's serious, that doesn't mean you have to take it seriously all the time. Fun is the nectar of life. Teach him to drink deeply from it whenever he can.

Big Guys

(7–11 years)

Big Guys are at the point where they're really starting to get to grips with the fact that communication is a powerful thing. Even if they don't use a lot of words, they will have a lot going on in their lives, and all of it will seem vastly important to them. The difficulty for us sometimes is that much of the stuff they come and tell us, or want to show us, might seem a little, well, trivial at times. The reason it seems trivial is obviously because a lot of it is really trivial.

Do we really always care that today in class Johnny Brown tipped his paint over and some of it went on the table, and Mrs Smith had to wipe it up, but then Johhny started crying, and so she had to get Molly to help him, but Molly didn't want to because Johnny had been mean to her at lunchtime and . . . blah de blah de blah?

No, we don't always care. Not if we're being really honest. Sometimes you might be busy getting dinner ready, or trying to finish something from work, and you may not always care about the details of Johnny's paint dramas.

What is important, though, is that you put the effort in now to show him that, as much as humanely possible, you are always interested in talking to *him*. Maybe the content is a little dull sometimes, but he needs to learn the lesson well that you're always interested in talking with him. None of us can do that with 100% consistency; God knows I struggle with it when I'm being told my 78th amusing Spongebob story of the day, but we should try as hard as we can. In just a few years time the tide will change and the conversations will dry up for a while, so now is the time to show him that you're there for him, and you're interested.

So my top three tips for Big Guys are as follows.

1 *Be interested.* I know it's hard sometimes. Just do the best you can so that he hits his teenage years thinking that his mum has always had a minute or two to listen to what he had to say.

2 *Teach flexibility.* This is also the time to really help him develop a flexible approach to his emotional responses to

things. Usually you can't do much in the middle of an angry patch except try to manage it, so save this for the debrief afterwards. Bedtime chats are a fantastic time to process an angry outburst, and ask him whether there was any other way he could have responded, or whether the way he thought about the situation was the only way to think about it.

3 *Teach confidence.* This is simple because all you have to do is tell him that you know he's a smart guy, and that he's quite good at figuring this stuff out. You also know that he's good at knowing his own feelings and not being pushed into feeling something unless he decides its best for him. You also know that he's a strong person, and he doesn't let his feelings push him into doing stuff that he knows is wrong.

This stage is all about building competence and confidence, and showing him that you are really interested in what's going on in his world. Some of it will be dull, but as I'm sure you've already discovered, there's loads of stuff that is hugely interesting when you set about discovering how Big Guys see the world.

Young Men

(12–18 years)

This is the bit where it usually gets tough for mums, because teenage boys can seem like quite odd creatures. It can be hard to understand how your lovely nine-year-old who used to give you hugs and cuddles has been replaced by a grumpy 14-year-old who acts as if you are simply an obstacle to his happiness. The words tend to dry up and are replaced with grunts, shrugs and sometimes even scowls. Usually it is this lack of communication that scares mums the most. The worst thing you can do at this stage is to try to talk your way out of it. Some mums make the mistake of thinking that if they just hang in there and keep talking for long enough, eventually he'll *have* to say something.

Nope. He'll just get more annoyed.

What you have to bear in mind here is that the average teenage boy is an arch pragmatist, which means he just doesn't see the point in talking. Why bother telling you about his day? It's already happened. Why bother telling you about his plans for the future? He either doesn't have any yet, or doesn't want to go on about them in case they don't work out and he looks dumb. Why bother telling you what he thinks? It's just what he *thinks*, so who cares?

The secret to getting through this stage of the communication road trip is so elegantly simple that it's easy to miss: *stop talking, and wait.*

That really is all you have to do: just stop chasing him, and wait. He'll come back; you just have to be patient. As a result, here are my three big tips for navigating the communication conundrum with Young Men.

1 *Give him space.* Don't crowd him with words. Give him lots and lots of space. He'll think about what you've said a lot more if you give him room to do that. Sometimes all you might do is ask a question and just leave it hanging. The more room you give him to think, the more he actually will think.

2 *Pragmatism is everything.* The key phrase that a teenage boy lives his life by is 'what's in it for me?' If you get that, then half the battle is won. When you talk with him, you'll probably find it a lot more effective to keep this concept in mind and always try to angle your conversations back to the advantage to him in what you're trying to communicate.

3 *Less is always more.* The most important thing to remember when talking to teenage boys is to use as few words as

possible. Don't use commas in your sentences, and use question marks as sparingly as you can. Short, simple, clear requests are best. The more words you use, the more opportunity you give him to start an argument.

I'm not saying that you shouldn't talk to teenage boys, because you should, but you need to pick your moments. In some ways you need to be a little like a Buddhist nun – not so much for the nun bit, but more the way that Buddhists approach the subject of teaching. You see, a Buddhist will never come up to you and start preaching. They wait to be asked first. If you do ask, then they will happily tell you all you would like to know, but they will never impose anything on you. You have to ask first.

If you use the same approach with your teenage boy, then your relationship with him will be a lot more productive, and he will listen a lot more. Don't preach to him: wait until he asks.

Sometimes you may have to wait a long time.

16

Lion-taming: managing boys' behaviour

For some mums, managing boys' behaviour can seem a bit like lion-taming. Boys can be noisy, fierce creatures and – even though this is totally normal, and fantastic fun – it can be a little off-putting sometimes. Again, the trick with boys is to understand their fundamentally pragmatic nature, because once you get that you'll see that boys are a far easier ride than they might at first appear. In fact, having now spent the better part of 20 years helping mums to find ways to better manage their boys' behaviour, I think there are really only a few very basic principles to remember (is it any surprise that I think there are three?) when you're applying all the basic tools like time out, sticker charts, taking his stuff away, grounding and the like.

The three basic principles

1 *Structure is vital.* Boys thrive in a structured world. They don't like anarchy, because that means you have to waste a lot of time and effort charging about trying to find out what the limits are. In my experience it doesn't matter if you've got a Little Guy or a Young Man, they always like structure. You don't want to go all over-the-top about it, because that just

gets painful and causes lots of arguments, but you do want
to give him enough rules and predictability in his life that he
knows how to navigate the day. They like rules, and they like
knowing how things fit together. The rules need to be kept as
simple as possible. Usually, I suggest that family rules should
be only about three to five points, an example being:

◊ Treat people and property with respect.

◊ Do agreed jobs within agreed times.

◊ Make mum cups of tea whenever she wants.

2 *Keep instructions simple and clear.* Don't over complicate
things. The point I made in the previous chapter about less
being more is hugely relevant here. The more words you use,
the more opportunity you present him with to turn it all back
on you.

3 *Always link action with consequence.* In keeping with the simple
and clear theme, it's important to always make sure that
there is a clear and unambiguous connection between his
actions and the consequences that flow from them. Don't just
expect him to get that: spell it out.

General tools of the trade

All the usual things work with boys just as well as girls. Sticker
charts are good for Little Guys because, for some weird reason,
Little Guys will do anything to get the sticker. Time out works as
well. Forget all the banana split you hear about time out, all that
stuff about never putting them in their room, or never putting
them in the hallway. Find somewhere they don't like and put
them there. Obviously we are not talking about a box with spiders
in it, because really all you need to do is put them somewhere
boring and that will do the trick. Some kids like being put in their
room, some kids hate it. You can also forget all that stuff about

one minute for every year of age as well, because some boys – like my own sweet son on one occasion – need anywhere up to 60 minutes for every year of age.

The Ladder of Certain Doom

If you've already read one of my other books you would have come across this, so feel free to skip this bit if you like. If you haven't, then let me briefly introduce you to my own little invention, a nifty little thing that I call the Ladder of Certain Doom. This works very well with kids in general, and seems to work particularly well with boys. The only prerequisite is that children need to be old enough to understand the concept of time. So this usually *won't* work with kids younger than six. Even if your kids are older than six years, you want to make sure they understand in a real sense the notion of time increasing and decreasing. We'll get to why it's good with boys in a minute, but first let me give you my standard spiel about how you use it.

8.00pm
7.30pm
7.00pm
6.30pm
6.00pm
5.30pm
5.00pm
4.30pm
4.00pm
3.30pm

1 Draw up a simple ladder on a piece of paper as shown right. The ladder starts at his normal bedtime and then goes down in half-hour steps until the time he gets home from school. If boys are younger, you can make the steps 10 or 15 minutes.

2 Put the ladder up on the fridge where he can see it.

3 Place a fridge magnet at the very top of the chart. The magnet now becomes the 'flag' that tells him what time he's going to bed. Each child gets their own distinctive magnet or 'flag'.

4 Every day starts with the flag at the top of the ladder –
8.00pm in the example above.

5 If there is bad behaviour, then the flag moves down a rung.
If the bad behaviour doesn't stop in a given period of time
(usually a 1-2-3 count), then the flag moves down another
rung.

6 Similarly, if you ask him to do a task within a set period of
time (best measured with the microwave timer) and it isn't
done, the flag moves down a rung.

7 The flag keeps moving down until your request is complied
with, or the flag reaches the current time and then he goes to
bed. If the flag gets to 3.30pm and it is 3.30pm, then off to
bed he goes.

8 **This next bit is very important:** If he has *lost* time off his
bedtime he can *earn* his way back *up* the rungs by doing a
payback job (see below).

9 Really good days, where he hasn't lost any time, are rewarded
with special treats, as are really good weeks. You should
decide what is a realistic number of good days to qualify for
a weekly reward for your boy. (It should be a bit of a stretch,
but definitely achievable. You might start with two good days
and gradually increase this as his behaviour improves.) In this
way, the ladder also doubles as a sticker chart.

Payback jobs

Payback jobs are fundamentally important to how the ladder
works. Payback jobs are the vehicle for getting out of negative
cycles and back into positive ones. The purpose of the payback
job is to encourage him to enter into positive behaviour. Some
examples of payback jobs are given below.

◊ emptying the dishwasher

◊ hanging out the washing

◊ tidying up the room

◊ hoovering

◊ doing something nice for the younger sibling he just
    hit

◊ feeding the alligator (obviously, close supervision is required
    with this task – children should never feed large carnivorous
    reptiles without an adult in the room)

It is important that he has a choice of which payback job he does:
choice increases the chance of compliance. I suggest that parents
have a small box of cards that children can choose from, each with
a separate payback job on it and the steps that each job entails.
An example is shown below.

Emptying the dishwasher
1 Carefully take each piece out of the dishwasher.
2 Make sure it is dry.
3 Put it away in the right place.
4 Close the dishwasher.
5 Wipe away any water on the countertop.

By establishing the exact components of the job, you avoid a
debate about whether or not the job is finished. The card acts as
an objective checklist: all you have to do is look at the card, look
at what he's done and then the answer is clear. If there is still
water on the countertop, you simply say: 'That's good, but you've
forgotten Step 5. Tell me when it's done, and I'll let you move the
flag up.'

The size of the job should be reflected in the size of the payback. So, for example, he might get to go up two rungs (one hour) for cleaning his room, and only one rung (half an hour) for emptying the dishwasher. This will depend on his age as well. When he completes the payback job, praise him lavishly and make sure he feels good for making the decision to get off the grumpy train and climbing back on board with the team.

Can the ladder be used with older boys?

Yes, it can. In fact I know of a number of schools that have implemented their own Ladder of Certain Doom with older kids. Also, in addition to all the normal mums and dads who have used the ladder, I have also seen it used quite effectively in group homes for teenagers. The trick is that with older kids you substitute early bedtimes for some other privilege, like curfews, time on the computer or time on the phone.

Why is it particularly useful for boys?

The reason I think this works well for boys is that there is a clear, easy-to-understand structure. What's more, there is an immediate link between what you do and the consequences of that action. In addition, it puts the responsibility on boys to manage their own feelings and behaviour. If he starts yelling and screaming, you don't have to do anything other than move the little flag down the chart. If he doesn't get himself under control pretty quickly, then he's going to lose out big-time. If he does, then not only has he complied with your request, but he's learnt the very valuable lesson that his anger doesn't control his behaviour, *he* does.

Most of all, never forget that he's a boy

This last point is a fundamentally important one when it comes to managing behaviour, particularly for mums raising boys by themselves. If there's a dad about he will remind you of this fact, and if he does you should listen. Many of the mums I see in my private practice make the mistake of trying to make their boy more like how they would *like* him to be, or how they think boys *should* be, rather than letting him be who he *is*.

They think that if they can just somehow instil in him a fundamental belief in the value of tidy rooms, quiet voices and gentle play, then he will come to see the light.

Sorry, but no.

You might be able to button all that stuff down and control him when he's a Little Guy, but eventually it will all spill out. And if he's spent the first part of his life living in a sterile, quiet, controlled atmosphere, then chances are when he hits his teenage years he'll overcompensate and set out with unbelievable determination to live in filth and grumpiness.

If you ever wonder about what's normal for boys, let me give you the main points just so you can be reassured:

◇ noise

◇ yelling

◇ pushing and shoving with siblings and friends

◇ fighting with siblings

◇ mess

◇ mud

◇ yelling

◇ playing with sticks

◇ violent games where people get shot, blown up and decapitated

◇ collecting insects

◇ obsessing about dinosaurs

◇ hoarding all kinds of old junk (treasures)

◇ grumpiness

◊ laughing

◊ yelling

◊ farting

◊ fart jokes

◊ toilet humour generally

◊ burping

◊ making fart noises

◊ fascination with dangerous, risky stuff

◊ more farting

◊ yelling

That's just a very basic list of all the things that are normal. None of these should alarm you or give you cause for concern. They simply *are*. In the last chapter I'm going to give you some suggestions for how to put this stuff into practice and be a cooler mum. Don't skip ahead, though, because that's cheating for a start, and we still have quite a bit of important stuff to go.

17

Crime:
when good boys go bad

*Inside every hardened criminal beats the heart
of a 10-year-old boy.*

Bart Simpson

We all want good boys, that's a given. Not many parents set out
wanting to create criminals. Some do, and I've met more than my
fair share of those, but most of us don't. I think it would be fair to
say, though, that most parents worry to varying degrees about the
risk of their kids going off the proverbial rails at some point. This
is compounded by the fact that most of us can remember that
we ourselves committed minor acts of delinquency and general
yobbishness when we were younger. Most of us probably didn't
rob banks, but we might have engaged in a little shoplifting,
maybe some petty vandalism?

What is more worrying is that there seems to be a universal
perception that youth offending is on the increase. It's hard not
to notice youth offending, because every time you turn on the
television or pick up a newspaper you see this stuff. Just in
the past few weeks I've seen reports about a 10-year-old boy in the
US who has just been charged with murdering his own father,
two 14-year-olds who have committed separate murders and

another teenager who is apparently in court today charged with torturing and then hanging a cat.

What the hell is going on?

A little bad is normal

Surprisingly, it turns out that being a delinquent is pretty normal, at least a *little* delinquency is normal. When you examine the crime rates from most Western nations around the world over the course of recent history, a remarkably stable picture emerges. It's probably of no great surprise that criminal behaviour peaks during adolescence, actually at about age 17, with teenagers making up the majority of criminal offenders, and then drops away fairly sharply into adulthood.

By the early 20s the number of offenders decreases by over 50%, and by age 28 about 85% of the former adolescent delinquents have stopped offending. This age-related profile is similar for boys and girls, and for types of crimes as well. Thankfully, most of us grow up, get a job and leave behind the nonsense of our youth.

It's important to really get your head around those numbers, because that might make you panic a little less if your darling boy is brought home by the local police. What's even more enlightening (or frightening, depending on how you look at it) is that the self-reported amount of criminal offending by adolescents is always far in excess of the official crime rates. Most teenagers commit some form of crime during those years, and most of them don't get caught. I myself was apprehended for a grand total of 0% of the criminal offences I personally committed between the ages of 13 and 21 years of age. Which is lucky for me, and I dare say for my poor old mum's blood pressure as well.

So the big message here – and it's a message worth remembering if the police ever do come knocking at your door – is that one conviction does not a hardened criminal make. I'm not saying you should brush it off as if it doesn't matter, because obviously it does, but you need to keep it in perspective.

The two different types of troublemakers

In my experience, there are two different types of teenage boys who get in trouble with the law. The first type is the classic idiot. This boy is not an idiot in terms of his basic level of intelligence – which can vary anywhere from really smart to really stupid – instead, it has more to do with the fact that his offending was an act of . . . well . . . just plain *idiocy*. I've met many, many boys who fit into this category. Good kids from nice families who just went out and did some stupid thing without really thinking too much about the consequences.

One clear example I remember is a young man who was sent to me for a second opinion about what treatment he needed, because he'd been arrested for exposing himself to a young mother and her three-year-old daughter in a preschool. What the genius didn't realise was that this particular young mum was married to a cop. She promptly got on the phone, and within about a minute the place was swarming with police cars. My young man was arrested walking away down the street laughing his arse off with a couple of mates. The handcuffs pretty much took care of the jovial mood.

Now, you might think at first glance that this young man was a deeply disturbed little puppy, but actually the reality was a little different. It turned out that he was with his mates and they'd seen this woman walking past on the way to dropping off her daughter. They'd thought she was 'a looker' and his friends had then dared him to go and expose himself to her, which, after a few minutes of teenage-boy macho bullshit he'd promptly gone and done.

He was staring at a year's worth of treatment and meetings and all kinds of carry-on. My view was pretty clear from the beginning. Flashing, or indecent exposure, is not a team sport. In fact, it is very much an individual pursuit. This is not something that adolescents, or adult men for that matter, go out and do in groups. This boy was not a sex offender; he was an idiot. He'd never been in any trouble before, and was otherwise a fairly typical teenage boy.

I met with the boy and his parents and did all my usual hoop-de-doo, then when all the relevant information had been gathered, I shared my theory with them: 'I don't think your son is a deviant,' I told them. 'I think he's an idiot.'

They looked pretty relieved, as I'm sure you can understand. I asked the boy if he thought he was an idiot, and he agreed that he was, on reflection, an idiot. After that we agreed that all the boy needed was for me to make sure he understood how that kind of behaviour can hurt people, and then the adults needed to decide on an acceptable punishment.

Not a bad boy. Not a deviant. Just an idiot.

The second group in my experience is smaller, and of much greater concern. This group I call 'bad buggers'. These are the kids whose offending isn't an isolated event, but instead is part of a long-standing pattern of trouble that started young and will in all likelihood, unless something pretty significant happens, continue until they eventually end up in jail. These kids aren't necessarily 'bad buggers' through and through, but you have to dig long and hard to find the remnants of the decent kid they once were buried deep down inside.

I have also, sadly, met a great many of these boys. There is something about these kids that is quite striking. There is often a brooding angriness about them, a darkness that far exceeds the usual teenage-boy grumpiness. It isn't about the intensity of the anger, but the depth that it has penetrated. It's like a stain that goes all the way down, a dirty grey smear that's so ingrained, it's like a second skin. These boys come with a file that is pretty thick as well. They usually have a list of troubles stretching all the way back to the beginning.

Fortunately, far smarter people than me have found a slightly better way of encapsulating that than simply breaking them up into 'idiots' and 'bad buggers'. In fact Dr Terrie Moffitt and her colleagues have looked at data from a sample of 1,037 babies followed up for over 35 years and found that there are indeed two different kinds of adolescent offenders: a group they called 'adolescent limited offenders' and another group they called 'life course persistent offenders'.

Adolescent limited offenders

These boys represent the vast majority of kids who commit crimes during adolescence. While this group commits about 50% of the total number of crimes, they are about 95% of the total number of adolescent offenders. This means that the vast majority of adolescents who commit crimes are in this group, which is good news because that means that about 95% of the teenagers who commit crimes will grow out of it.

The reasons these boys commit offences are most likely pretty varied. For a start, we know that teenagers tend to be impulsive and, while they can make good decisions, that ability to make good decisions starts to decline pretty rapidly as soon as their mates are around. It's also pretty clear that a lot of adolescent offending is about macho bullshit, trying to impress either your friends or some girl. Peer groups generally can have a big influence on whether or not you get into trouble. If your peer group includes some boys who are of the life course persistent type, then you're a little more likely to get into trouble than if your peer group includes boys who want to be lifeguards.

Like I said, all kinds of reasons, but again the key thing to remember is that 95% of teenagers who break the law fall into this category, and 95% of them grow out of it.

Life course persistent offenders

Just the name of this group suggests that things aren't looking so good for them. On average, these boys represent about 5% of the total number of offenders and have a history of antisocial behaviour that stretches all the way back to childhood. These aren't the boys who were a little bit naughty in preschool; these are the kids who got expelled from preschool. 'They will be biting and hitting at age 4, shoplifting and truancy at age 10, selling drugs and stealing cars at age 16, committing aggravated robbery and rape at age 22, and fraud and child abuse at age 30.' The nature of what they do as they grow up will change as they have new opportunities to create mayhem, but the fundamental nature of the mayhem will remain the same. What is amazing is that research has fairly consistently shown that this small group of somewhere around 5% of the total number of adolescent offenders is responsible for an incredible 50% of all the crimes in every city and country.

These boys are quite different in terms of their backgrounds as well. The fact that they show signs of delinquency as far back as their preschool years suggests that the causes have to be present either before birth or shortly after. There are all kinds of possible suspects here, from maternal alcohol and drug use, to early deprivation and neglect, poor post-natal nutrition, child abuse and possible genetic factors. The search for why these kids are the way they are continues, and it's likely that a range of causes might one day be identified.

It's also worth noting that, while these boys tend to come from lower socio-economic groups and families where there is significant dysfunction, not all of them do. I've worked with boys who would fit into this group very nicely who came from what appear to be normal families with normal parents. Life is a complex thing.

Whatever the case, it is pretty clear that this small, determined group of boys pretty much seems to hit the ground running. They are very different to other boys from a very early age. This is not to say that biology trumps life experience. Dr Moffitt and her colleagues took the view that, while it is likely that there are subtle neuropsychological dysfunctions that these boys arrive with, or acquire shortly after birth, this doesn't mean they're necessarily damned to a life of crime. Instead, the argument – and I think it's a pretty bloody compelling one – goes that we need to identify these children early and put substantial resources into assisting them during those vital early years. If we do that, then there's a good chance we can prevent them from falling off the edge into a life of crime.

Interestingly, the New Zealand Government recently announced their intention to screen all children before age five to identify those who were most at risk of developing these kinds of life course persistent criminal outcomes. I was amazed that politicians were suggesting something that was not only completely supported by some very substantial research, but what's more was actually very sensible and might actually make a real difference.

This announcement was met with the inevitable wailing and gnashing of teeth by the civil liberties types, who were appalled that children were going to be labelled as criminals at such a young age and put on some sinister government database. They didn't want any part of a scheme that they said would label children as criminals from as young as three. 'All children should be treated equally,' they wailed.

I was, sadly, not in the least surprised by that reaction.

Rather than identifying and helping the children at most risk of developing significant lifestyle problems that would in all likelihood lead to later ill health, trouble with the law, prison sentences and general misery, we should treat all children as if they're the same. Instead of acknowledging that such children exist, that their needs are very real, and that their outcomes if left to fend for themselves are grim, we say these children who are most at need should be treated as if they were same as any other child.

Thank God the civil libertarians were there. It is all too often true that ideology trumps common sense in these enlightened days we live in.

A brief note for the overly anxious

At this point I feel compelled to point out the obvious, which is that just being a bit naughty, or even quite a bit naughty, does not make you a life course persistent offender. I always struggle when talking about this group, because, while it may well help a significant majority of mums to feel a little more relaxed about the fact they almost certainly have an 'adolescent limited' variety, there will always be a hard core of anxious mums who worry that they will have a life course persistent type. The truth is that, with a prevalence of around 5% in most developed countries, if there were a meeting for mums whose kids have got in trouble then about five in 100 would have one. The very, very good news is that this also means that 95 out of 100 mums don't: their boys will do a few stupid things, and then grow up and get on with their lives.

What to do with good boys who go bad

So what do you do if you have a boy who is getting in trouble? Well, there are a number of things you can do, and I'm going to lay it all out for you now. I should say, though, that I'm talking here about what you can do if you have the adolescent limited (or 'idiot') type of boy. The life course persistent boy is a whole different kettle of fish. If you have one of those, you no doubt are already involved with a large number of professionals. If you're not, you should be. And if you are and it isn't helping, then tell them that; and if they still can't help, go find someone else who can. Keep trying until you get to someone who can help you survive raising one of these kinds of boys.

1. Don't panic

This is important, because chances are that if your boy is in some kind of trouble then panic will be only a whisper away. So the first, most important thing to do is pause, take a breath and clear your head. The worst thing you can do is to screw it up at the very beginning by jumping right in and reacting before you know what you're actually reacting to.

Take a moment – take two, for that matter. Find out what's happened as coolly and as calmly as you can. Ask very short questions. If you don't get any answers, don't wade into him. He's probably a little stressed himself at this point, and he's going to be looking for a way to deflect the attention from him. Having an argument with mum about 'fussing' is the perfect smokescreen. So don't get baited into a fight. If you have to, say nothing and count to 10. The big thing here is to remain calm, focused and in control. If you aren't: fake it. If you can't: then remove yourself far enough away so you can vent a little, then get back in there.

Above all other things, the start is not the time for feelings. You can have feelings later, but when it all first kicks off reacting to your feelings will just make it worse.

2. Don't get too angry

You notice I didn't say 'don't get angry'. Only an idiot would say don't get angry, because you're going to be angry. Again, though, if he is in trouble, then either he's going to be looking for a way out of the spotlight (in which case getting into an argument with you will do very nicely) or he's feeling genuinely bad and genuinely stressed about what he's done (in which case getting angry isn't necessary).

So when can you get angry? Basically, once you've taken care of business. Once you know he's OK, that everyone else is OK and that there is a process in place – be that with the school, or the police, or whomever else might be involved – then you can get angry. You *should* get angry at some point, because if you're completely cool about it the whole way through, then it gives him the message that what he did wasn't that big a deal. If you don't get angry with him after he punches some other kid, or damages something, or steals something, then it's a lot harder for him to get the message that you are disappointed and disapproving of what he's done. You should be disappointed and disapproving, and he should know that.

Just don't get *too* angry. There's a big difference between letting him know that you're upset about what he did, and grinding him down into the ground. Yelling and screaming isn't going to achieve anything other than letting you blow off a bit of steam.

3. Let him feel the consequences fully

There is a real temptation, because we love them, and because their happiness is more important than our own, to bail our kids out of trouble. Don't do this. I've seen what happens when parents bail their kids out of trouble, and it isn't pretty. I can understand it, completely, because I have boys of my own, and if they were in trouble I'm sure there's a large part of me that would want to do whatever it took to get them out of a jam. I'd like to think, though, that I wouldn't do that.

Sometimes the most help you can be to them is to let them take the fall. Better that they take a small – or even medium-sized – fall now than a much bigger one later on. If he does something wrong, he has to pay the consequences for it. He needs to understand that ultimately he is responsible for his own actions, and the only way you can teach him that is to let him *be* responsible for his own actions.

If you teach him that Mum or Dad will dig him out of a hole each time he's stupid enough to jump into one, then you're not being a good parent. One day you will be too old or too dead to pull him out. You want him to learn that in life we all dig our own holes, and we all have to climb out of them on our own as well.

If he is given some kind of punishment – be that a curfew, or community service, or some form of reparation – make sure that he does it, and if he doesn't, or won't, don't you do it for him. I am constantly amazed at how many boys' parents will do their boys' punishments themselves just to try to stop him from getting in any further trouble. If it's *his* punishment, then it's *his* punishment. If you do it, or pay it, or sort it out for him, then you're letting him down. Your job is not to bail him out; your job is to help him see the connection between his actions and the consequences that flow from it.

4. Seek wise counsel, not clever counsel

If you are at the point where you need some kind of help or advice, choose wisely. If you are going to see some professional like a psychologist or a counsellor, do your homework. Ask around for recommendations – local police youth aid people or social work offices can often give you the best recommendations. When you go see them for the first time, ask all the questions you want to and make sure that you're completely comfortable with them. Trust your gut on this one: if it doesn't feel right, go find someone else.

There are a couple of things to remember if you're deep enough in the doo-doo that you need to choose a lawyer. The first and most important thing you need to bear in mind is that lawyers like to win. I've met some really great lawyers over the years who represent young people, and I've met some wallies as well. If you choose a lawyer whose only interest is in winning, you might still end up losing far more than the current battle: they may well get your boy off when really that's the worst thing that could happen. If he did it, then he did it regardless of whether some clever lawyer can get him off.

Similarly, you don't necessarily want a lawyer who is going to blindly advocate for the lightest punishment they can get. Again, sometimes a light punishment is a bad thing. Sometimes you want the punishment to actually outweigh the crime.

With the distressing tendency for parents to involve lawyers in all kinds of disputes at school, it is doubly important to stop and think about the message that you are giving your son. By all means we should fight injustices, but that doesn't always mean that everything is unjust, or that involving a lawyer is the best way to sort things out. We'll talk about this more in the education section, but for now let me say that you should be very careful before you set your lawyers on anyone on your son's behalf.

5. Model respect: never bad-mouth the police, the court, schools or anyone else in front of him

Sometimes you might feel that your son has been unfairly treated, or perhaps even deliberately picked on. At such times you may feel very angry at whoever was doing the picking, and might feel the urge to say something unkind about them. Don't. Not ever.

The very worst thing you can do for your children is to model disrespect for the police, the courts or school. The people who make up these groups are the first and often last line of defence between us and total bloody anarchy. In all groups there will be good people and not-so-good people. There will be people who are fair, and even-handed, and who genuinely strive to help the people they come across; and then there will be others who are bigoted, biased, short-tempered and sometimes just plain mean. I've met some great cops, and some not-so-great cops. I've seen kids who were treated fairly and kids who were not. What I have *never* done, and will never do, is bad-mouth cops, judges or teachers in front of kids.

We need to model respect for the institutions that we charge with keeping the public order. We might not always respect some of the individuals in those institutions, but we must always model respect for the institution itself. If we don't, then we're giving our boys the message that it's OK to mouth off at the cops, or teachers, or judges and the like. Generally, in my now-fairly-extensive experience in this area, mouthing off at a cop tends to end badly a significant amount of the time.

6. Compassion is good; idiot compassion, not so much

The term 'idiot compassion' isn't mine, but actually comes from a Buddhist monk, Trungpa Rinpoche, who made the very valid point that we should all have compassion for people who make mistakes; however, continuing to have compassion for someone who keeps knowingly making the same mistake over and over again is simply idiot compassion. As parents we are predisposed to idiot compassion, because we want to believe the best of our children, and we desperately want to believe them when they appear genuinely sorry and express an apparently genuine desire to change.

It's important if he does screw up that your boy knows you are on his side. This doesn't mean that you excuse his behaviour, or even that you believe everything he says. Surprisingly, a great many boys will lie to their parents when they've done something wrong. Just as surprisingly, many parents make the mistake of believing their boys with no real analysis or investigation.

'If he says he didn't do it, then as far as I'm concerned he didn't do it' is something I've heard many times. That kind of blind faith in your boy is at once touching and a bit naïve. Finding the right balance between believing in him and being naïve is a difficult one. The only help I can offer you on this one is: try to find out as much as you can that is incontrovertible fact, the stuff that doesn't rely on opinions, and then you simply have to make a call. You might get it wrong, but them's the breaks. If you are wrong, fess up, change your plan and move forward.

By all means have compassion for your boy, have it in buckets, and barrels, and spare paper bags. Just don't have idiot compassion, because there is bugger-all dignity in it.

Some examples of how not to handle things

I thought it would be useful to provide some very brief examples of cases I've been involved in where parents have handled things less than wisely. It has always been my experience that the best learning comes from mistakes, and it's far less painful to learn from other people's mistakes. You might shake your head and tut-tut a little when you read these, but I would suggest that a little humility is warranted. More often than not, what we think we'd do and what we end up doing in situations such as these are not always the same thing.

Kane, aged 14, burglary and causing intentional damage

Kane had been arrested for breaking into a neighbour's house with two friends. The boys had completely trashed the house and done thousands of pounds worth of damage. They'd smashed things, written on walls, and one of them (although they all denied it) had peed all over the neighbour's bed. Kane's version of events painted himself as the innocent bystander who kind of got swept along by the other two. He said that he hadn't really wanted to go into the house in the first place, but his two friends had really wanted to go trash the place so he'd gone along, albeit reluctantly, to make sure they 'didn't get too out of it' – something hotly disputed by the other two boys. There was some history between Kane's family and the neighbour as well. Essentially, the neighbour would get very annoyed that Kane and his mates would sit out in the backyard playing loud music and swearing like a bunch of sailors on shore leave.

What his parents did

Basically, Kane's parents lawyered up early on and took the attitude that their job was to believe their son, and the police and the neighbour's job was to prove exactly what he had done. They were antagonistic with the police, and defensive when talking with me. They didn't see why their son should be singled out when there were two other boys involved. When I pointed out that he wasn't being singled out, they said that they still felt that he was. Their lawyer was very good at her job, and Kane got off with a very light punishment. Basically, he had to do 20 hours' community service at his dad's factory, which I'm pretty sure involved him sweeping up for about an hour or so and then sitting cruising the internet for the rest of the time. At home, despite all the money his parents had spent paying for their very good lawyer, and the reparations they paid to their neighbour on Kane's behalf, he remained rude and generally quite painful.

The advice they ignored

1 Fire the lawyer, or at least muzzle her.

2 Make Kane apologise to the neighbour.

3 Ground him until the reparations have been made and his community service has been completed.

4 Sell his stuff to help pay the reparations, make him work off the rest.

5 Deal with his behaviours at home and make him understand that behaving like a snot isn't an option unless he is prepared to go find his own place somewhere else (which at age 14 pretty much leaves only foster care as an option).

6 Once he's done all that, he can start earning back his
   freedom, and their trust.

Tom, aged 11, swearing at his teacher

Tom was quite bright, and the oldest of three boys. He had always
been 'spirited and independent' according to his parents, and had
been getting into minor trouble with one particular teacher for
most of that year. On the day in question, Tom had been working
on the computer in the classroom and the teacher had asked
him to finish off his session and return to his desk. He ignored
her. She asked again. He ignored her again. She asked him a final
time. She turned the computer off and asked him to go pay a visit
to the deputy head. Tom, bless him, told her to fuck off.

What his parents did

During the meeting with the deputy head and Tom later that
afternoon, Tom's parents expressed some dissatisfaction with
Tom's behaviour, but focused fairly extensively on Tom's teacher's
abilities. They said that they felt she did not understand Tom's
particular needs. He was very bright, they said, and they felt that
the *real* problem was that Tom wasn't being stimulated enough.
They said that, given Tom was so high-spirited, it was inevitable
that if he became bored he would act out. Surely, they helpfully
suggested, it would have been wiser for the teacher to leave Tom
on the computer, because he clearly found that more stimulating
than the class activity that the teacher had planned. In the end,
after much arsing about, Tom's parents removed him from the
school and placed him in a private school that they thought
would more adequately cater to his particular needs.

The advice they ignored

1 Make him apologise to his teacher, and to the deputy
   head.

2 Together with the teacher and the deputy head, work out what an appropriate punishment should be.

3 Explain to Tom that, given this was his first offence, he would just have to do the school's punishment, but that if anything like that was to ever happen again he would find that all the joy, stimulation and material possessions in his life would be quickly sucked out.

4 Make sure that he understands that being bored isn't an excuse for telling your teacher to fuck off.

5 Meet with the teacher to try to work out how they can work with her to best ensure Tom's behaviour in school improves.

Jamie, aged 16, aggressive and threatening behaviour at home

Jamie was being raised by his mother, his dad having left when Jamie was only two years old. He'd been a good boy up until about a year before, when he had taken up with a couple of boys whom his mum thought were a bit dodgy. Since that time, things had been getting worse and worse at home. It was as if he suddenly didn't give a monkey's about his mother, and seemed to think he was suddenly the man of the house. He was belligerent, rude and arrogant, treating the family home as if it were just a dosshouse. He would stay out until late, and then return home drunk and smelling of dope. Whenever she asked him where he had been or what he had been doing, he would get angry and start to scream abuse at her. Over recent months, the verbal abuse had escalated and become physical. He'd started throwing things at her, and had pushed her over and punched her in the arm hard enough to leave a major bruise. Finally, his mother had called the police one night after he'd threatened her with a knife. He hadn't used the knife on her, but he'd made it fairly clear amid a stream of expletives that that would be the logical consequence if she did not shut up and let him do what he wanted.

What his mother did

Jamie's mum loved him dearly, and ultimately he used that against her. She started off strong and followed through with pressing charges. She also signed him into the care of social workers until he could get his act together. Jamie was placed in a foster home that he hated. It was run by two very experienced caregivers who didn't take any shit from anyone. They'd been looking after wayward young men for decades and had the measure of Jamie as soon as he walked in the door. This was why he hated it so much: because they knew exactly what game he was up to, and there was no way they were going to be bullied like his mum. He ran away once, but the police caught him and brought him back. His mum attended family therapy sessions and seemed to be getting it. With the benefit of a little space, she began to see how much of a bully he had been and what she needed to do. Just when it looked like all was going well, Jamie ran away again, and this time he made it all the way back home. He cried. He told her that the other boys picked on him, and that the caregivers were mean. Through blubbery, repentant sobs, he promised her that he would be good, that he'd stay home, that he'd follow the rules, that he'd never verbally or physically abuse her again. She gave in and didn't send him back.

The advice she ignored

1 Send him back.

2 Send him back.

3 Send him back.

Hayden, aged 14, shoplifting

Hayden had been caught stealing a magazine from the local supermarket. He was caught by the store's security guard, and the police were called. He hadn't been in trouble before, and it was a relatively minor offence, so the police and the supermarket people were happy for him to write a letter of apology and issued him with a trespass notice. A month later, he was caught stealing a CD from another store; two months after that, he was caught stealing a pack of batteries from another store.

What his parents did

Basically, not much. He kept stealing stuff, getting caught, writing letters of apology and getting trespass orders taken out against him. They couldn't understand why he kept doing it, and wondered if it might be ADHD. His parents, who were both very busy people, kept up their busy lives.

The advice they ignored

1 Wake the hell up.

2 Get Hayden's attention by taking away everything that he owns in the world. Strip his room of everything he has until it is but an empty shell.

3 Every week that goes by without him stealing something, he gets to choose five things he can have back.

4 Spend some time with him.

5 Spend a bit more time with him.

6 Find out what he's interested in, and spend a little more time with him doing that.

The secret to having crime-free boys

See, now that's a bit of a trick heading, because as we've seen almost all boys engage in some kind of criminal activity. To be sure, there are some boys who completely abstain from any kind of criminal activity, but they're a very small group. Oddly, there's been very little research looking at this group, so we don't know much about what's going on for them. My guess would be that they're probably fairly mature lads, who have taken on fairly mature roles, and are involved in groups or organisations that provide a good outlet for the recklessness of young men, while at the same time providing structure and supervision.

Having said that, there are boys I've seen in my practice who were just like that and still got into trouble for doing something really dumb.

Idiocy can strike anywhere, anytime.

18

Drop-kick dads

While it is true that there are many *great* dads out there, it is also true that there are more than a few drop-kick dads. To be fair there are just as many drop-kick mums as well, but they won't be reading this book so there's no point in me going on about it. Having said that, I'm sure some irate bloke out there will take offence at the title of this chapter and send me an email having a crack at me for slagging off dads. I'm not.

I had a dad myself, and he was great. I'm a dad as well, and – most of the time – my boys think I'm great. Objectively, they don't have any other dads to compare me with, but regardless of that fact they still think I'm great for a statistically significant percentage of the time that we're together.

I'm *not* having a crack at dads generally, because I think that dads generally are doing a pretty good job. I *am* having a crack at drop-kick dads, though, because I've seen far too many of them, and I get a bit tired of their excuses. My view is that if you're a parent, you do whatever it takes to be there for your kids. If you choose to opt out of their lives for whatever reason, then you're a drop-kick.

There will, however, be quite a few mums reading this who are having to help their sons deal with the harsh reality of having a drop-kick dad. This can be a heartbreaking thing for a mum to have to deal with, because no one wants to see their son hurting, and there is no doubt that a drop-kick dad can cause a great deal of hurt.

A tiny soapbox moment

I've spent a number of years doing assessments for the Family Court in custody and access cases, and over that time I've seen an awful lot of people, both mums and dads, who seemed to have an awful lot of trouble putting their children's needs over their own needs. Many times I've wished that somewhere in the Psychologist's Rule Book there was a clause like the following:

> *1.2.4 (d). In situations where it is clear to the psychologist that the parent being assessed for the Family Court is in fact acting like a selfish, petulant child, and further when the psychologist believes that the parent is projecting their own unresolved feelings about the other parent onto the child, and then using this as a justification to use the child as a ping-pong ball to score points off the other parent, the psychologist is permitted to give the parent a bloody good slap and instruct them to 'grow the hell up', 'put their own shit aside' and 'do their damn job'.*

Unfortunately, there is no such provision, so I was always forced to restrain myself. There were times when it took great effort to do so. I have sat with mums who were convinced that the father of their children was a total drop-kick when it was my clear view that he wasn't. He may have been less than perfect, but he was trying his best and genuinely wanted a relationship with his son. In those situations, usually what was going on was that the adults didn't like each other, and they each thought their relationship with each other somehow reflected the nature of each of their relationships with the kids.

I have seen otherwise sensible people, who should have been able to reach a perfectly amicable solution, waste years of their lives, and the bulk of their property settlements, on lawyers and endless petty squabbling in the Family Court. All of which means that the backdrop to the children's lives is conflict and argument.

My advice to people is to do everything you possibly can to prevent it getting to the point where everyone is lawyering up and heading to court. No one wins then. All you've done is swapped arguing in person for arguing by way of affidavit, all of which are being typed by people you are paying hundreds of pounds an hour.

Do *anything* and *everything* you can to avoid being one of those people. No one wins – even if you 'win' in court you've still lost, because you've wasted a lot of time and money and goodwill. Most of all, your kids lose when their parents can't stop fighting.

If you do end up in that situation because your partner is hellbent on a scrap, then play a straight game, even if the other person isn't. The rules for playing a straight game are incredibly simple.

◊ Never bad-mouth the other parent in front of the children.

◊ Keep all conflict away from the children.

◊ Unless there are genuine safety concerns, work hard to ensure that the children have an opportunity to develop a relationship with the other parent, even if you don't like it.

◊ Don't enlist the children to gather information about the other parent.

◊ Keep the information you give them about what is

happening as neutral as you can. You want to be honest with them in a manner that is appropriate for their age.

◊ Always try to take weight off their shoulders, not to put more on.

◊ Always remember that your emotional relationship with your ex may be finished, but your son will have an emotional relationship with his father for his whole life.

Sometimes mums are in the situation where they are doing their best to stick to the rules but dad isn't. Sometimes you can be playing a straight game, while he's playing a nasty, undermining, intimidating, unpleasant game. There's nothing you can really do about that, except to continue playing your half according to the rules. It might be easy for him to fool his eight-year-old son, but one day that boy will grow up and give you both a score for how you handled the separation. If you played straight, you get a high score and you get a relationship. If he didn't, then his son will score him accordingly. Your boy will be an adult much longer than he's a child, and one day he'll see through all the games and nastiness. Just make sure that when that happens you are on the right side.

Diagnosing a drop-kick dad

In my experience, a drop-kick dad can usually be spotted by various combinations of the following telltale signs.

◊ Simply walks away and abandons his son outright.

◊ Abandons his son but claims that you won't let him see him, when in reality you've done everything you can to make contact possible.

◊ Makes all kinds of promises to come for access visits and then doesn't turn up.

◊ Makes all kinds of excuses about why he didn't turn up when he fails to turn up.

◊ Doesn't visit, when the judge has made a specific ruling about contact, because he didn't get all the things he wanted in the agreement.

◊ Says that he won't see his son until he does get all the things he wants in the agreement.

◊ Refuses to have contact with the children unless contact is unsupervised, in cases where the judge has decided that there is a risk to the children's safety and so has granted supervised access only.

◊ Claims any kind of moral high ground, principles or higher powers as being a reason for him not seeing his son.

◊ Blames your son for the lack of contact, saying that when the boy can show he's willing to make an effort then *he* will make an effort. Often this will be accompanied by blaming you for doing such a crap job of raising him in the first place.

◊ Blames you outright, and says that the reason he wants no contact is because you're such a bitch.

◊ Starts a new family somewhere else and says that it's probably best for everyone if you all just go your separate ways.

Of course there are slightly less extreme versions of this as well, but these can be no less painful. A dad doesn't necessarily have to completely abandon his son to be a drop-kick. There are lots of dads who, while not abandoning their sons outright, abandon them in other more subtle ways. There are dads who might see their sons, but pay them no attention. They might physically be in the same room together, but that is where it ends.

How to help your boy

There is no magical answer to this one, but I do have a few suggestions from having seen far too many boys over the years in this same situation. Some of these may help you with your boy.

One good mum can make up for a hundred drop-kick dads

I have seen time after time how the presence of a good mum can make up for the literal absence of a drop-kick dad. What your son needs most is a good parent – and if you're there, then he's got one. His dad not being there is going to hurt him, and he's going to have to find a way to sort out what he thinks about that, but that fact that you are there is a treasure beyond value.

Don't be afraid of his feelings

Sometimes mums worry that when their boys are quiet, or angry, or crying that this is always a bad thing. None of us likes to see our children hurting, and when they do, it hurts us. It can be very easy to start to worry that these feelings are signs that he is about to fall apart. The truth is that it really sucks that his dad doesn't want anything to do with him, and that can sometimes make him feel sad, or angry, or both. Getting upset about it isn't a bad thing at all. It just means he's paying attention.

Let him know that you know it sucks

It does, so why pretend any different? This is hard, because you don't want to run down his dad even in this situation. You're pretty justified to do so, and you could probably get away with it: just don't. You never know when his dad might come back into his life, and maybe later on it could be just what he needs. So even though you probably want to bad-mouth him for hurting your boy, don't. What you *can* say is that not having his dad around sucks, and that you understand that.

Tell him that his dad is the one who's lost the most

One of the ways that you can help him to get his head around what his dad's missing out on is to put it in a different frame. This is how you might explain it to him: 'I know that it really sucks that your dad isn't part of your life, and I know you really feel like you're missing out on a lot because he isn't there, but do you know who lost the most? Your dad. See, he's missing out on seeing you grow up. He missed when you were five and all your friends were over and we had that Spongebob cake. And he missed when your first tooth fell out, and when you got that prize in football, and the first time you went away on a school camp, and the first time you did an olly on your skateboard, and all that stuff. He's also going to miss saying goodnight to you tonight, and good morning to you tomorrow, which makes me feel very, very sad for him. One day he's probably going to wonder about all those things, but by then it'll be too late because he's missed it all. You're such a great kid, and he's missed out on all of that incredible stuff. Watching you grow up is a miracle, it's a treasure, and he's missed out on the whole thing. Most of all, I just feel sorry for him that he missed out on all that great stuff'.

Or something like that.

Let him smash stuff

Sometimes when you're a boy, you just want to smash stuff. I had an email from one mum who said that one of the things she did was to give her son a sledgehammer and let him go out and smash up some old cars in their drive. It was messy, and noisy, but from time to time he'd go out and pound on the cars for a while, and that seemed to make things better.

Ask him what he's learnt about himself

The old proverb about how the things that don't kill us make us stronger is a good one in my experience. It can be a useful thing in some quiet, well-chosen moment to ask the question: So what's all this stuff made you learn about yourself? One of the things about we humans is that we have a tendency to find meaning in just about anything. Some time reflecting on what he's made of all the stuff with his dad can be useful. If he does think it's all his fault, he just might tell you, which means you can then talk about it. You might be surprised, though, because he just might have learnt some positive things as well. You'll never know unless you ask.

Teach him that problems aren't excuses

This one really comes back to that core value of responsibility. Having a drop-kick dad is no excuse for treating other people, especially you, badly. It's fine for him to get upset, and angry, and all the rest, but it is not fine for him to take it out on you. It's not your fault that his dad left, that was his decision, so don't let phantom guilt trick you into becoming your angry boy's punching bag (either literally or metaphorically).

Have the wisdom of granite

The wisdom of granite is simple and profound: things work themselves out in time. Be patient and give him time. If you're doing all the other things that mums do, then he'll get there in the end. You'll probably have many moments along the way where you are filled with all kinds of doubts and fears, but just remember the wisdom of granite. Be patient, have faith; things work themselves out in time.

Male role models

Kelly was recently separated, and her son, Brody, was just turning six. Brody's dad, Steve, had come home one night and told Kelly that he'd decided he needed some space because he felt suffocated by the whole 'family thing'. He packed a bag and left that night. Apart from a couple of visits and a phone call, he'd basically abandoned Brody as if he were a project that had simply become too boring to bother finishing.

Drop-kick, I thought to myself.

'So how're you all doing?' I asked her.

Kelly shrugged. 'I'm better. It was really hard at first, because I didn't think he was the type of guy to just walk away like that. I kept expecting that he'd come back, but then as time went on it became clear that he wasn't coming back. Then I heard he was seeing someone else and I knew it was time to make the break.'

'So what'd you do?' I asked her.

'I dropped Brody at school and then piled up outside all his stuff that he hadn't collected yet and told him to come get it.' She smiled sheepishly, 'It was raining pretty hard that day, so he got over there pretty quickly.'

'Nice,' I said, meaning it and returning her smile. I don't have a lot of sympathy for people who abandon their kids.

'Yeah,' she said. 'He was pretty angry and hasn't spoken to me much since then.'

'Ah well, you know how the saying goes: into every life a little rain must fall.'

She smiled.

'So what's brought you along to see me?'

Kelly sobered up quick as a blink. 'I'm really worried about Brody,' she said.

'How so?'

'I'm worried that he doesn't have any strong male role models in his life. I don't have any male friends or any brothers, and all his teachers are female as well.'

And there it was: the eternal issue of male role models. If there is one single thing that mums going it alone worry about, it would be that one. What impact will growing up without a dad have on their son?

When dad's not there

The first thing to understand is that, while studies do show that boys do particularly well if they live with both parents, it isn't just as simple as having a dad physically present in the house. What really matters is having a *good* dad. Living with a drop-kick dad is very bad for boys. Exposure to domestic violence and parental conflict has been shown, time and time again, to have a very negative impact on all children's well-being. So if you were living with that stuff and you got your boy out, good on you. That's what good mums do.

Similarly, the simple fact that a father is absent from the home isn't the defining issue in how children do following separation and divorce. There are a host of factors that contribute to how boys do over time that are far more important than the simple presence of a male in the house. What we also know is that one of the most important factors in a child's resilience (that is, their ability to deal with stressful life events) is the presence of a supportive relationship in childhood. It doesn't matter who provides that relationship, just so long as the child has at least one of those in his life. So as long as your boy has got you on his side, he's just as well-equipped as anyone else to deal with what comes along.

Does he need regular contact with male role models to learn how to act like a boy?

I don't think anyone could argue that having good male role models isn't a good thing, and I'm certainly not wanting to say that. Most mums do everything they can so that their boys get to spend some time with good men. The question is: what does it mean for your boys when they don't have access to good men? This is certainly the case for a lot of boys in a world where divorce and separation are part of the landscape.

How does he learn how to 'act like a boy' if he doesn't have regular contact with a man who can teach him how to do 'man stuff'? The good news is that it doesn't seem that he needs to have regular contact with a male role model to learn how to be a man. In fact, studies have shown that there is no difference in gender role behaviour (the scientific way of saying 'man stuff') between boys who grow up in a two-parent house and boys who grow up with a single mum. So you can relax about that one. He'll get his man stuff from everywhere and nowhere – you can't walk about in the world and not see man stuff.

There are lots of boys who grow up without the assistance of male role models. While it's great if you have access to some good guy who can spend some time with your boy, don't worry about it too much if you don't. The most important thing is that he's got *you* in his life, because, as I said, one good mum can make up for a hundred drop-kick dads.

After the various world wars, there has been a bit of a shortage of fathers. Now while I'm sure it was rough for those kids growing up without their dads, they still did. Somehow the world kept turning. Life is a complex, multifaceted thing, and to hang too much on whether or not your son has a male role model is selling yourself way short.

I know there are loads of people – particularly people writing in the area of what boys do or don't need – who would disagree with me about that. That's why you read so much about the importance of having male role models. It sounds good, and it makes a certain degree of sense. What you always need to keep in mind, though, is that just because something sounds good and seems to make a certain degree of sense doesn't make it necessarily *true*.

What boys need are *good* role models, and it doesn't much matter if they're male or female. We know that children tend to choose close relatives as their role models, and that boys in particular also look to popular-culture figures like sportsmen and actors. Obviously as he enters his teenage years, he's going to look more and more towards other men to see how to be, but that doesn't mean that those men have to actually be living in your house, or even be part of your daily life. He can find the sportsmen and actors all over the place for the man stuff.

Luckily, he also has access to a great role model every single day, someone who's known him since the day he was born, before he was born for that matter. Someone who's been there through all his victories and his defeats. Someone who, by lucky coincidence, lives just down the hall. You.

Introducing your new 'special friend'

A difficulty that lots of single mums also face is how to introduce a new partner, be it a new guy or a new girl. While the latter is probably much easier, the principles are the same in both cases. These are my top tips for bringing a 'special friend' into your boy's life.

◊ *Wait until it's serious enough to warrant the potential stresses it might cause.* There's nothing to be gained from introducing every guy/girl you date. Usually all that does is cause problems when he sees a whole lot of new people coming and going.

◊ *Slow is best.* It's just plain old common sense that the best approach is a softly-softly one. Introduce the newbie with caution, and understand that everyone is going to need time to adjust.

◊ *Get clear about the roles with your new partner.* The newbie isn't a new dad, and shouldn't act or even think like that. The newbie is the newbie, and should be treated with the respect given to any visitor in the house, but no more. Anything else has to be earned. Make sure your new partner understands that you are the parent and that it will likely be quite some time before they get voting rights.

◊ *Be prepared for a reaction.* It's likely that your boy is going to find it difficult having someone new come into the family, particularly someone he might feel is trying to replace his dad. Both you and your new partner need to be prepared for this.

◊ *Be tolerant, but don't be a punching bag.* Your boy might get angry or upset, but he still needs to show you the same respect he always has. You have a right to a life of your own, and he's going to need to understand that and accept it. This might take a while, so in the meantime let him be angry, but not rude.

You do have a right to your own life, because one day your boy will be gone and you'll be watching telly by yourself. Most boys have a problem with someone new coming into their mother's life, but that doesn't mean you should avoid relationships or hide them.

19

School

Education is, without a doubt, becoming increasingly important in this hyper-connected e-world that we live in. The past 150 years have seen changes that are so amazing, we've all become completely ho-hum about the whole thing so that our brains don't explode. See, my theory is that if we all really thought about the amazing stuff that's gone on over the course of even our lives, we'd pop, and to avoid this we've developed a shield of benign disinterest.

Just as a little experiment, let's clock your reaction to the following.

◊ With the advent of global positioning systems, cars can now know more about where they are than the person driving them.

◊ During the 2008 US presidential elections, I watched a live hologram of one of the Black Eyed Peas (a band for those of you not in the know) talking live from the park in Chicago where President-elect Barack Obama would give his victory speech.

◊ If I knew your address, I could log on to Google Street View and take a virtual stroll down your street. My office is at

7 Bond Street in Dunedin, New Zealand; go look me up if you'd like. We're up on the second floor by the fire escape. The fact that you can sit at home and go for a walk down the road I work in is amazing. The road itself isn't all that amazing, but the virtual strolling is miraculous.

◊ Machines made by people have landed on the moon, collected rocks on Mars, and even as we speak some of those machines are at the very edge of our galaxy heading out into deep space.

◊ There are steak knives that can cut through metal cans – and, what's more, if you buy one set, they give you another one free.

All that stuff is pretty damned incredible, and things are just going to get more and more amazing. As I write this book the world is in the grip of an economic crisis that's changing the courses of all our boys' lives. The world changes, and changes, and changes again, and all we can do is try to keep up.

So what about our boys? How best can we help them? We've seen so far that there does seem to be a gap between how boys and girls are doing in school. How much of that is real, and how much of it is how we test things like reading and writing and maths, and even how we statistically analyse those results, are up for debate. Some people have interpreted the apparent gap as boys being in 'crisis', while others have said it's just that girls have been making progress faster than boys.

As you know, I'd clearly place myself in the second camp. I don't think there is a crisis in boys' education, so much as there is a crisis in *some boys'* education. It makes complete sense to me that *some* boys are in trouble in school, but it seems a nonsense to make global statements about *all* boys being in trouble. I've got two of my own and they both seem to be doing fine, as do the vast majority of the other boys in each of their classes.

So bearing all this in mind, how do we each help our own boys to do as well as they can in the education system? In this chapter I'm going to run through each of the stages and suggest some ways that you can best help your boy to get the most out of school. These things aren't prescriptions; they're just suggestions, a general pointer about some possible places to start.

The preschool years

These are the Godzilla years, and so the most important thing to remember is that his primary goal at this point in his life will be driven by his Godzilla-like tendencies.

◊ The most important thing during these years is warm, consistent-ish care. No one can be consistent all the time, but we should strive for consistent-ish.

◊ Routines and boundaries are good for little boys. In my experience, kids with routines and boundaries are happier than kids who live in a more chaotic environment. This doesn't mean that you let the routines dictate every last moment, but you just aim for enough structure to give life a little predictability.

◊ Fun is the order of the day here when it comes to learning. They don't need to learn baby sign language or how to write their name by age three; instead, what they need to learn – and what you need to reinforce their whole life – is that learning is fun. It's just fun.

◊ Whatever you do, don't become one of those dreadfully intense, insufferably boring mums who want to turn every last little thing into a learning experience. That can suck the very fun out of living, so don't be one of those people. You won't make him smarter: all he will learn is that you're a real drag.

◊ Don't choose preschools on the basis of which ones provide the most structured learning environment. Don't choose a preschool on the basis that they guarantee he'll be reading two years above his age by the time he starts school, or that he'll go straight into an accelerant maths programme. Choose a preschool on the basis that you like the staff, that the facilities are good, that the other kids look happy, that generally the place gives you good vibes and that he's going to have *fun* there. The main task of the little boy is, simply, to be a little boy.

◊ He also needs to learn to play co-operatively with other kids, and to develop a sense of empathy for people around him. Remember that he's only a little guy, so we're talking about rudimentary empathy here – things like don't hurt or annoy other people because they don't like it, be good to people and they'll be good to you, look after your friends and all the other rules of how to get along that we want them to learn.

◊ Fun. Mostly just let the boy have fun.

The first day of school

The first day of school is a big day, not just for him, but for you as well. Truth be told, you'll probably find it harder than he will. More tears are shed by mothers on the first day of school than by children as a general rule. It is, after all, one of the tangible signs that your little baby is now a little boy, and that the long process of leaving home has begun.

Starting school is when he starts to develop his own life, his own friends and his own secrets. From that point on, we are increasingly visitors in our children's lives. It is also usually the first time they will be cast adrift in a sea of children without an adult watching their every move.

This is a tough day for a lot of dads as well, but generally we are a little more philosophical about it. I had my fair share of anxiety on my elder son's first day, but I was excited for him as well because I knew that grand adventures of one kind or another lay in front of him.

His mother cried.

I don't mean to belittle her response at all – because she also was genuinely happy that these were the first real steps he would take setting off on his own life – but mothers feel a special pain of separation on that first day of school.

'Oh well,' I said as we drove off, 'at least it's going to be nice and quiet until three o'clock from now on.'

I am happy to report that after the initial traumas of separation faded for her, within a few days she came around to my way of thinking and has remained there ever since.

What I'm a little bemused by is how much of a production the first day of school has become. It seems like the 'transition' to school is beginning earlier and earlier and takes longer and longer. There are now multiple school visits prior to the big day, and parents staying for hours – and sometimes days – as a way to gently ease our dear wee lads into being at school.

My view is that a lot of that is a bit excessive. I know that many teachers find that the presence of parents in the classroom for extended periods can be distracting, and many teachers I speak to about this roll their eyes and smile politely.

It's just, you know, a bit silly.

I'm all for transitioning kids into school, because it will make the start of school way less stressful; but the bigger deal you make of it, the bigger deal you make it into. In my experience this is especially true for boys who are anxious about starting school, because your parents only ever tend to hang around if there's a chance you could get really upset. Just the presence of a parent suggests to the boy that there's something pretty big going down that might be so upsetting that his parents need to hang around.

So, for what it's worth, here are my generic starting-school suggestions.

◊ Start talking about school early, not in a big fussy kind of way, but more in a 'won't it be cool when you're a big boy and can go to school' way.

◊ If you know which school he'll be going to, point it out from time to time as you drive or walk past.

◊ Maybe go there at the weekends to ride a bike or kick a ball around. Don't make a big deal out of being there, because the only thing you're trying to do is get him comfortable in the environment.

◊ Once you clock past the fourth birthday, you can start to bring it up a little more. A good way to talk about it is in that vein of 'won't it be exciting when you're a big boy and . . .' type of thing.

◊ A few months out, introduce the idea that soon he'll get to go out and choose his schoolbag and lunchbox. You need to make this into a real rite of passage thing. In the days of the cavemen, boys probably went out and killed their first mammoth, but because we have no mammoths you can substitute choosing a schoolbag and a lunchbox.

◊ School visits are fine, but you don't have to do a thousand. In most cases one or two is fine. Again, the tone should be more a kind of low-key anticipation than a 'how do you feel' vibe. He will look to you to try and understand how he should be feeling about it all, so if you get excited about his big day, then he probably will too.

◊ On the night before the big day, lay out his new stuff and run through the next morning. It's important to tell him that you will drop him off at his class and that you will stay for a little while because it's all very exciting and you want to watch him having fun on his first day, but that you won't stay for long because you know that big boys like to get on with their first day at school by themselves.

◊ On the big day, keep it all low-key and even. Take photos and videos if he's keen. If he's not, then sneak them while he isn't looking, because he'll want to look at the photos one day.

◊ When you get to school, walk in with an upbeat tone. Help him to stow his gear, and then hand him over to the teacher. Stay for a little bit, but then once he's starting to get wrapped up in the morning give him a wee wave, and a kiss if you think he's cool with it all, then quietly exit.

◊ Don't cry until you get out of the classroom.

My view has always been that we want to create in our kids a sense of mastery and confidence. If we act as if starting school is so enormous and traumatic that they will need us there holding their hand and mopping up little tears for hours and hours, then I don't see that as being very helpful. I don't want my boys to think that I don't believe they can cope with the big things. I want them to know that I believe absolutely that they can cope with the big things.

Not everyone has an easy start at school, however, and sometimes the road to independence is paved with tears. If your little guy has trouble settling in, you'll need to work with his teacher to get it sorted. What you should not do is stay simply because he gets upset. He may be clamped in his teacher's arms and crying his little heart out, but you should still leave. He will calm down, and most new entrant teachers are well-experienced in dealing with upset kids. If you stay, all you'll do is validate his anxiety and feed the tantrum.

Leave.

My older son had a couple of mornings like that when he started school, and I left him in tears and broken-hearted on a few mornings. I felt like a heel, second-guessed myself all the way, and was sure he would hate me. Still, I'd told hundreds of other parents to leave, so I could hardly chicken out when it was my turn. I left, he dealt with it and now he loves school.

Little hearts break easily, but they mend incredibly easily as well.

The early school years

(5–10 years)

The good news about the first few years of school is that it isn't really about what you should do, but what you shouldn't. I'm assuming here that you're not dealing with a wee bloke with specific learning needs, but instead just have the bog-standard wee bloke who might be good at some things and not so good at others. In that light, here's my list of don'ts.

◊ Don't get all anxious and over-the-top about learning.
  For most of us, learning happens at its own pace if we don't get pushed. The problem is that some mums get so wound up about learning that they make learning a grinding bore.
  It isn't about being in the top reading group or the top maths group, what it's really about is helping kids to see that the act of learning is one of the greatest things there is.

◊ Don't interrogate him about his day at school. You're going to want to know, but, for reasons that are hidden to the rest of us, it seems that secrecy is part of the little guy code. Many questions about what happened today, and how the day went, are met with shrugging and muttered variations of 'stuff' or 'I can't remember'. The best time to ask little guys stuff is when they're walking. The process of moving their legs in a walking fashion often distracts them so much that they don't seem to notice they're actually telling you things about their day.

◇ Don't solve every problem for him, academic or social. It is part of the nature of things that problems will arise, both in class and with other kids. It doesn't help him if you simply march into school and sort everything out all the time. Part of how we learn to deal with problems is to deal with problems. This doesn't mean that you leave him to deal with everything all by himself; instead, what you do is that you sit down and try to figure out what he can do to get it sorted, and if that doesn't work then you can look at whether or not you need to go in and talk to his teacher.

◇ Don't go in and talk to his teacher about every last little thing. They will never say this, but they're busy people and they get a little bogged down by some of the relatively trivial things parents often want to come in and talk to them about. By all means go and talk to your teacher if you are genuinely concerned about something, just try to remember they don't get paid very much and they have an awful lot to do.

◇ Don't go in and rescue him if he gets in trouble. If he gets in trouble for being naughty, then he has to sort that out and deal with it. Far too many parents (and a lot of them are mums) wade into school whenever their precious little one gets in trouble, complaining about how it isn't fair, or it wasn't their son's fault, or the teacher wasn't listening to him, or some other waffle. If he gets in trouble, he should take his punishment. Sometimes it might not be his fault, but all that means is that he has a valuable early opportunity to learn that life isn't always fair.

◇ Don't EVER run down the school or the teacher in front of him. He needs to learn that the school and the teacher must be respected. You can't bad-mouth the school or the teacher and then expect him to behave. Remember that he looks to you to see how to act.

Probably the most important thing to do during these early years of school is to try to encourage his love of learning. Everyone loves to learn, we just don't all love to learn the same stuff. Your main job at this point is to help him to experience the thrill of learning some new thing. It is in the nature of boys to become obsessed with different things over time. Dinosaurs usually feature in there somewhere, as do animals, bugs, machines and a hundred other possibilities. Whatever his current thing is, that's how you can help to show him that learning is fun. He doesn't have to be learning his multiplication tables all the time to be learning about numbers. You can do that with Lego blocks or spiders' eggs or anything.

For example, if you find an enormous black hairy spider in the garden, you could ask him how many eggs a spider lays. If he doesn't know – which he probably won't –then you can either make a number up or go look it up on Google. Then you can figure out how many brothers and sisters this spider will have. Actually, calculating the number of huge black hairy spiders in your backyard may be a little creepy, but the upside of this is that most little boys love creepy, gross stuff.

The difficult teen years

(11–19 years)

These are the years which can take years off a poor mother's life. The stakes are getting higher just as any semblance of reason often seems to disappear from the landscape of their personality. For all the reasons we discussed back in Chapter 1, communication in most teenage boys is pared down to the bare minimum required for survival. Just when you want to know more about what's going on with them at school, they get to the lowest ebb in the conversation tide. They don't want to tell you much about what's going on because, being arch pragmatists, they don't see the point. They also believe that if they tell you anything you'll just ask more questions, so best just say nothing. For what it's worth, these are my suggestions to help you get through this somewhat stressful time.

◊ You're going to need to start to come to terms with the fact that from this point on he will essentially be running his own life and making his own decisions. Some of these decisions will undoubtedly be bad ones, but that's life. More importantly, it's *his* life. This is where you really start to let go.

◊ You must play a delicate balancing act during this period of his life. On the one hand, you want to be encouraging him to study, and making sure that he understands that it's an expectation you have that he will do the study that's required of him. And on the other hand, you need to give him enough space to do it in his own way. There are no magic answers to this: just do the best you can.

◊ Encourage some kind of routine, and do whatever you can to help him build a place to study, wherever that might be. If he wants to listen to music, let him listen to music. I did when I studied, and studies have shown that boys prefer to listen to music more than girls do. It doesn't have to make sense to you, it just needs to work.

◊ Most boys leave things to the last minute. They exercise the completely reasonable rationale that there's no point in doing something early because, you know, the world could end on Saturday, so better off to wait until Sunday night to finish the assignment. Sometimes even first thing Monday morning. Many adult boys work to a similar strategy. For myself, I don't know if it's true that I work best under pressure because I have no comparison. I *only* work under pressure. Generally I don't start writing a book until I get a cold, panicky feeling in my gut when I look at the number of days I have left between the dates on the calendar and the date on my contract. Many of the women I say that to shake their heads in disbelief. They struggle to understand why you wouldn't get it done well ahead of time. Men just nod and go 'yeah'.

◊ Don't rescue him if he gets in trouble because he hasn't done something. It's the same principle all the way across the lifespan: the way you teach responsibility is to let him *take* responsibility.

◊ Don't do his assignments for him.

◊ Don't hassle his teacher for extensions to deadlines. He needs to understand that it's *his* problem to sort out.

◊ Similarly if he gets in trouble at school for his behaviour, don't ride on in and sort it out. It's his trouble – let *him* sort it out. For example, if he's getting picked on by a teacher who doesn't like him, then he needs to learn to be extra careful around that teacher.

◊ If he's mucking around and won't study and acts like he doesn't care, then there isn't much you can do apart from let him experience the consequences of his choices. You can't make him study if he won't. He might fail, he might get kicked out; that's very possible. It can be traumatic for a mother to watch her incredibly bright and talented son fail his way out of school, but some boys have to do that before they find something interesting enough to make them want to study. He might pack grocery bags for a while, but you just need to trust the fact that if he really is bright, then eventually he'll get bored with manual labour and find another way back into the education system. There are many boys who take a winding road to the mountain; not everybody travels down the straight and easy highway.

◇ Remember the wisdom of granite. We all have to find our own place in the world, and invariably we all do. Sometimes this is a straightforward process, and sometimes not. You just have to trust that, assuming you've done all the early stuff about values, and morals, and manners, he'll work it out for himself.

The biggest challenge of these years is working the balance between encouragement/expectations and letting him have the space to figure out his own way. The smart thing is not always the obvious thing; sometimes the wisest course might be to do the opposite of what you might actually want to do.

When I was 17, I left school on the basis of a horoscope. I got up one morning, flipped open the paper, and when I looked under Cancer I read: 'today is a good day to do something you have been thinking about'. Now, I need to point out that I don't believe in horoscopes, not even a little bit. I didn't then and I don't now. It is a load of hippy poppycock in my humble opinion. Having said that, I was 17 and looking for any excuse to get out of school. I turned to my mother and said, 'Mum, I think I'm going to leave school.'

My mother, who is a far wiser woman than I ever gave her credit for when I was a teenager, simply asked me why.

'My horoscope says that today is a good day to do something I've been thinking about . . . and I've been thinking about leaving school.'

She paused for a moment. 'What are you going to do? Just sit around?'

'No, no . . . I'm still going to university at the start of next year, but I've got all the marks I need to get accepted, and I'm not doing anything at school anyway, so I'll just get a job and work the last six months of this year.'

'OK,' she said. 'If you've thought it through, it sounds OK to me.'

I was flabbergasted. I never thought she'd agree to me just dropping out of school. I'd suggested the idea just as a bit of a joke, never thinking she'd agree.

I don't know if she knew what a huge impact that conversation had on me, but it did. In many ways that was the moment I left childhood behind; that was the precise moment when my mum said to me that I was no longer a boy, and that she trusted me to run my own life. She could have got into a big argument with me and made me stay at school, but instead she checked out my thinking, and then told me she trusted me to do what was best.

That conversation changed the way I thought about myself, because I suddenly got the fact that I really was running my own life now. In a blink, I suddenly started to take everything a whole lot more seriously. It was a gear-changing moment in my young life, and one I still remember clearly almost 25 years later.

I hope that when that moment arrives with my own sons, I'm smart enough to figure out what we're *really* talking about, and wise enough not to screw it up.

The easy bit

(20 years onwards)

Nothing about parenting is all that easy, but this is about as easy as it ever gets. From this point, he really is running his own life. Your job now is to sit back and have a bit of a rest, and then start getting on his case about grandchildren. The biggest issue most mums have here is letting go. This is the point where he really is in control of his life, and the decisions he makes are his to make. As a result, I've only got three bullet points for this stage.

◊ Don't hover about anymore, the time for that – if there ever was one, and I'm of the view that there isn't – is long gone. You must not visit his lecturers to plead on his behalf (don't laugh: some mums do), and you must not negotiate or mediate in any way with his boss when he gets a job (again, don't scoff – because some mums do).

◊ Do enjoy the fact that his time has come to steer the ship fully and completely.

◊ Do give him advice if he asks for it, but always remember that the aim of the game is the same as it has been since he was little: to foster a sense that he's capable and able to handle things by himself.

He's going to make some mistakes, and some of them might be big ones, but that's all part of the ride. Now's probably about the time you should plan a holiday to somewhere warm and peaceful. If not, maybe just a movie and a coffee afterwards.

Bullying

This one is a struggle for all parents, not just mums, because no one likes to think of their kid being bullied. It's important, though, to first distinguish between real bullying and 'modern bullying'. Real bullying is the old-fashioned kind of bullying, where an older or stronger kid picks on a smaller, weaker kid. This is very bad and can make kids' lives a misery.

'Modern bullying' is mostly evident in little kids, and basically involves one kid doing something to the other kid that they don't like much (such as shoving or yelling at them), which then gets labelled as 'bullying'. This is more a case of modern children getting a little whiny and expecting the adults to resolve what are actually quite normal childhood disputes.

For example, my son came home one day and told me that he and his friend had been bullied by some older kids at school.

I bristled, but remained calm. 'What did they do?'

'They threw dirt in our eyes.'

Now, at this point you can bellow with rage, jump in the car, head down to school and demand action . . . or you can ask a few more questions.

'How did that happen?' I asked.

'Well, we were running round and round this tree they were playing beside, and they told us to go away.'

'And did you?'

'No.'

'I see, and what happened next?'

'Well, we kept running round and round them, and then they picked up some dirt and threw it at us.'

'In your eye?'

'Yeah.'

'So what did you do?'

'We ran away.'

'And did they chase you and keep throwing dirt in your eyes?'

'No.'

'So they just threw the dirt at you when you wouldn't go away and leave them alone?'

'Yeah.'

'That's not bullying, son. That's big kids showing little kids what happens when you're annoying them and you don't stop when they ask you to.'

'But they shouldn't throw dirt in our eyes.'

'No, they shouldn't. But how can you make sure that doesn't happen again?'

He thought for a moment. 'Not annoy the big kids?'

I nodded. 'Here endeth the lesson, son.'

See, if I'd waded into school and demanded retribution I would have ended up looking like a twit, and I could have made it far worse for my boy as well. Instead, I asked a few more questions, discovered it wasn't real bullying but instead that it was 'modern bullying', and sorted the problem out.

Real bullying on the other hand is a far more serious matter.

There is no doubt that the effects of bullying can be long-lasting. Apart from all the studies that show the way this stuff affects kids – and there are more than enough for me to be able to say that science is on my side – I've also seen first-hand, time and time again, how bullying can have a serious impact on kids' lives. So if it's real bullying, then you need to get involved early, but tactfully.

How you handle things will obviously be heavily influenced by your boy's age. With little guys, a visit to the class teacher can be all it takes. With bigger guys it can be a bit more complicated, because obviously there are issues of 'saving face' to be considered. One doesn't want to gain a reputation for running to Mummy to sort out one's problems, even if that's what one is doing. Schools are now expected to have anti-bullying programmes in place, and to have robust policies for dealing with bullies. As a result, once you've ascertained from your boy what has been going on, then you will probably need to meet with the teacher and/or head teacher as a first step. At this point, the things you will need to know would flow along the following lines.

◊ How is the school going to keep your son safe from the current bullying and/or being picked on more if the other kid(s) find out he has reported them?

◊ How will the bullies be dealt with? What remedial steps will be taken with them?

◊ How will the situation be monitored to ensure that the issues have been addressed?

◊ How will the school communicate with you about the outcomes of any investigations and/or interventions? Clearly there are confidentiality issues that the school is bound by regarding the offending pupil(s), but you should at least get some general feedback about outcomes.

If you can't get convincing answers to these questions, keep making noise until you do. If things have got to the point where you're having a sit-down meeting with the school, you need to be reassured that the school will be putting things in place to address both your son's concern and your own concerns.

The palm-heel strike and other options

On one occasion my younger son, only five at the time, was given a bit of a thrashing by another boy when we were out at a social occasion. We didn't see it happen, and he only told us about it when we got home. I asked him what the other boy had done to him.

'He punched me.'

'Where?'

'In the stomach.'

'And what did you do then?'

'I tried to punch him back,' he said, making a wee fist.

I shook my head. 'Son,' I said, 'I *never* want to hear about you punching anyone. *Ever*. It's wrong. Do you know why it's wrong?'

He looked at me for a minute. 'Because it's not good to hit people?'

'Kind of,' I said. 'It's not good to hit people first, but if they are hitting you, then it's OK to defend yourself. So why do you think it's wrong to punch people?'

'Because you could hurt them?'

'Nope. If they're hitting you, what you want to do is hurt them so you can get away. The reason it's wrong to punch people is that you can hurt your knuckles. What you want to do is use the heel of your palm,' I said, holding my hand up and showing him. 'If you use the palm-heel strike, you can slow him down without hurting yourself.' We then spent 10 minutes or so practising the basic technique.

So is it OK to teach a five-year-old that if he's getting a thrashing from another kid, he should step inside the other boy's punches and deliver the strongest palm-heel strike that he can to the other boy's stomach? Abso-bloody-lutely it is.

Your first defence is to run, your second defence is to try to talk your way out of it, but if it's come down to bare knuckles, then you need to be able to defend yourself. I have absolutely no problem with teaching children how to defend themselves, none at all.

The world is not always filled with people who want to discuss how their actions are making you feel, and other ways they could choose to interact with you other than smacking you on the side of the head.

Options, is all I'm saying; your boys need options when the other guy decides to get busy.

I have suggested to many, many parents that they take their sons, and their daughters, to basic self-defence classes. In particular, I'd recommend anything that teaches full-contact self-defence. Some of the Karate-type approaches look great but aren't as practical as something like Ju-Jitsu or, if you're lucky enough to live somewhere where there is a suitably qualified teacher, the fairly formidable Israeli school of self-defence, Krav Maga. Clearly being surrounded by millions of people who hate them has motivated the Israelis to develop an utterly pragmatic self-defence school.

What you will find in any reputable self-defence school is that the first suggestion will invariably be that if it's at all possible the best thing to do is run. They don't want to teach people how to get all Rambo: Runbo is usually far more sensible. The message here is that it isn't about teaching kids to be aggressive or violent, but rather how to protect themselves from that. The other positive spin-off is that if your boy knows how to handle himself, he will project that and bullies will tend not to pick on him. It is in the nature of the bully to target weaker kids, so why not give your boy the skills to push back if need be?

Besides, boys love that stuff.

If your son is the bully

For most parents our first response when our children are set upon is to defend them. It's natural, but not always helpful. If the school calls you in for a meeting and accuses your son of being the bully, take a breath before you react. Take several if you need to. I've seen more mums than I can count who leap to their son's defence when it is pretty clear that their son has been being a complete shite. You do him no favours by blindly believing him in the face of compelling evidence to the contrary. Basically, you need to listen to the evidence calmly, and then make a judgement about who you believe. Keep in mind that it is not uncommon for young men to lie their arses off to save themselves. Although schools can overreact, and sometimes simply get it wrong, they're generally a little more honest than your average schoolboy.

If you accept that he is at fault, it isn't the school's job alone to sort the problem out. I'll talk about working productively with schools in the next section, but at this point you should be thinking of behaviour problems at school as a team pursuit.

My suggestion where your boy has been the bully is that there needs to be an appropriate punishment, and an apology. The apology must be face-to-face, and if it was my son I would want to be there to make sure he did it genuinely and respectfully. Your boy also needs to get the clear message from both you and the school that if he does this again, there will be even more serious consequences. Your part of the consequences can be making sure that you remove every bit of fun he has in his life until he learns to treat people with more respect.

Working productively with your boy's school

There are some basic do's and don'ts when you're dealing with schools. I've worked with a huge number of schools, and so I've got a pretty good idea of what works and what doesn't. You mostly need to remember that schools have to deal with a huge amount of silly nonsense from overanxious parents. They field complaints about everything you can think of, and some things you probably couldn't, and being only human they do get a little sick of it. So here's my list of ways you can build a good relationship with your boy's teacher and school.

◊ Don't complain about every last little thing that happens. In a school full of kids, stuff is going to happen, and that is completely inevitable. Some of that stuff your boy is just going to have to deal with himself, or get over it.

◊ Don't make excuses for your son if he's done something wrong. Whatever you do, *never* say, 'Well he doesn't behave like that at home.' They won't believe you, and they'll only think you're an excuse-making parent. Just don't say it. Ever.

◊ Back the school, both when your son is there, and when it's just you and the teacher.

◊ If there's a problem, do everything you can to demonstrate to the teacher that you want to work with the school to fix it.

◊ Then do everything possible to fix the problem.

◊ Don't make the teacher piggy-in-the-middle if some other parent gets all in a flap about something your son has done and you think it's unwarranted. Take it on the chin and move on, although it's a good thing to tell the teacher that that's what you're doing so that they don't become piggy-in-the-middle.

◊ Don't be one of those painful parents who hang around and talk for ages after class with the teacher. They're busy people and just want to get their stuff done so they can go home. They'll never say that, but it's true. They don't mind a quick chat, and it's good to stay in touch and get to know each other, but *quick* is the operative word.

◊ Generally be understanding of the fact that teachers have to
deal with a lot of crap from kids, and even more from parents.
Don't be one of those mothers. Be the cool, supportive,
no-hassles mother. That way, if your boy does get into strife
you'll have a solid relationship already in place with the
people who can help you the most.

And one last quick thing

If your boy isn't doing all that well in school, and here I'm talking
about young men of the school-leaving age, then you might think
the best thing is simply to pull him out. In fact, it seems that
staying in school has an important protective effect for boys, even
if they're not achieving very much academically. Just the fact that
he's in a structured school environment can play a significant role
in keeping him out of more serious trouble, so, if it's an option,
try to keep him hanging in there as long as you can.

20

Extra-curricular activities

Money, horse racing and women,
three things the boys just can't figure out.

Will Rogers (1879–1935)

In Stephen King's fantastically scary book *The Shining*, later made into a pretty good film by Stanley Kubrick, the possessed and increasingly demented Jack Torrance sat in the empty ballroom of the isolated and haunted Overlook Hotel that he was looking after over the winter, and typed out page after page of the same sentence: 'All work and no play makes Jack a dull boy.' It was supposed to be Jack's great novel, but the bad stuff in the haunted Overlook Hotel got inside his head and it all ended in tears.

And axes.

Now, despite how things ended for the fictional Jack Torrance, he did have a point: all work and no play does make you a dull boy. I once saw a young man who came to see me because he was stressed. He was 16 and his mum had made the appointment for him. When I asked him why he'd come to see me, he said that he was having trouble sleeping because he was so stressed.

'What are you stressed about?' I asked him, given that it seemed like a reasonable thing to ask.

'I can't figure out how I'm going to fit in drama.'

I looked at him, slightly puzzled. 'Eh?'

'I don't know how I can fit drama into my timetable at school.'

'You're serious?'

'Yeah, serious.'

'How old are you?'

'Sixteen.'

'Dude, you need to goof off more.'

Maybe not the advice his mum was hoping I'd give him, but it was good advice nonetheless.

All work and no play doesn't just make you dull, it actually makes you dead before your time. You don't even have to be stuck in a haunted hotel for that to happen. Chronic stress will do that all by itself. In that light, a few extra-curricular activities are a good thing.

Mostly.

What I'm going to do in this chapter is cover off all the major extra-curricular pursuits of boys, the good, the not so good and the really not good ones.

Sport

I have to say that I'm not a big sports guy, not personally anyway. There are all kinds of really good things about sports for boys, but I've just never been really interested in it all that much. In fact, I've somehow managed to get all the way through my life thus far without ever having played sport of any kind. It's also pretty tough being a bloke in a sports-mad country. I couldn't tell you the name of a single person on any of our national sports teams and so I've spent most of my adult life bullshitting my way through sports conversations.

'What about that game last night?' someone will say to me.

'I know,' I'll reply, when in fact I have no idea what the hell they're talking about. 'What was that about?' which I say with an inflection that could be taken as either triumphant or incredulous disappointment.

'What about that second half?' the other guy will say.

'I know,' I'll reply, bullshitting all the way. 'Hard to believe.'

Hard to believe, indeed.

What has amazed me most of all is that I completely love going to my younger son's sports matches. My older boy has inherited his father's boyhood disinterest in sports, but my little guy is quite the wee sports nut. This was my chief fear when we had kids: that I'd get a sports nut and have to spend hours standing around bored out of my tree. I went along to his first football match feigning interest but expecting absolute boredom. It was thus an exceedingly pleasant surprise to find out that it was bloody good fun.

So the first big message here for non-sporty mums is that I've been where you are, sister, but get ready for a surprise, because there is nothing better than seeing your little guy all kitted up and heading out onto the pitch. And when he gets a goal, or scores a run, or catches the other guy out, the feeling is better than anything you've ever had before. Very, very cool.

And what's more, that moment when he scores the goal and then looks over to see if you're watching – that moment is a precious treasure for him beyond words. Little guys can grow a foot in a single glance.

There are also some pretty obvious health benefits from being involved in sports, particularly in an age where kids are increasingly couch-bound. In a recent study, researchers looked at 10,316 children aged two to six years in seven different countries and found that only 54% of them were doing the recommended minimum amount of exercise of 60 minutes a day. Boys were found to be doing more exercise than girls, but there's not much comfort to be found in simply beating the girls when such a high number of kids aren't exercising enough. Add onto that the escalating incidence of childhood obesity around the developed world, and you can see why sports involvement is a pretty good thing.

Another good thing about sports is that, chances are, you're going to have your kid involved with a group of kids who are likely to be a better influence than the kids who simply roam the streets.

Having said all that, don't feel that your boy has to play sport or he'll somehow miss out on fundamental boy stuff. As I've said in other places in this book, boys can find fundamental boy stuff anywhere. They can find it under rocks, in storybooks and piled up on old boxes. They won't grow up damaged if they don't play sport. There are lots and lots of good things about playing sports, but it isn't compulsory and it won't be the end of him if he doesn't ever join a team. It has also been my direct experience that whether or not he's going to want to play will be entirely down to him. If you're a sporty person yourself he's more likely to, but ultimately whether he does or doesn't sign up for the team is more down to his inclinations than yours.

Play

Play is hugely important, not only for boys, but for all of us throughout our lives. Your job as a mum is to make sure your boy gets plenty of play, and to give him the freedom to get up to his armpits in boy play. One of the great problems with modern parenting, at least in my opinion, is that we oversupervise and overinvolve ourselves in our children's lives. Many mums have become reduced to cruise-ship entertainment directors, with their little ones expecting a constant stream of stimulating activities.

It is *not* your job to keep your boy constantly entertained. Not when he's a little guy, and not when he's a big guy either. You are not the entertainment director you are his mum. It's *his* job to find something to do. This is not to say that you don't do anything with him, because you absolutely should do stuff with him, but you don't need to fill in every waking moment with things to occupy him.

What you should try to do is let him play like a boy. And how is that? A very clear example is a birthday party I observed with six four-year-old boys. There were a host of party games planned, but what happened is that the wee men spent two hours charging around the house hitting each other with plastic light sabres. They stopped briefly for chocolate and other nutritious party snacks, and then went back to racing around and whacking each other. The party was duly declared the best ever by all who attended.

As a general rule, boys like rough, noisy, messy stuff. If it's slightly dangerous, then that's best of all. Some mums struggle with the idea of boys playing with toy guns and swords. What you need to understand about that is that guns and swords are fun. F-U-N, fun. Playing with toy guns when you're six does not mean you'll grow up to be a violent criminal. I'm on pretty solid ground when saying this, I think, because, of all the thousands of truly violent criminals I've assessed over the course of my career to date, I have never had one tell me that he decided to become a violent criminal at age six when he was playing cowboys and Indians with his brother. Besides, if you don't give him toy guns, he'll make them out of pencils, or bits of wood, or the broken-off legs of his sister's Barbie doll.

He also needs to climb trees, build bridges over streams and throw spears. All of these things are good for boys. Dirt and the occasional bloody knee are important as well. The idea is not to let him recklessly do things like climb power pylons, but instead to play with the world in a relatively controlled way so that he can do things which might scare him, but which probably won't result in any serious injuries.

I think that one of the things I feel the most sorry about for boys growing up today is that they won't have enough good scars to tell stories about when they're older. My generation was allowed to go out and get ourselves some decent scars, but many of my son's generation barely manage to graze a knee.

As boys get bigger, their play gets bigger as well, which also means that the risks can sometimes get bigger. In my view it's important that you let him learn about risk when he's little, so he'll be better equipped to manage real risk when he comes up against it. If he broke his leg at age eight falling out of a tree, and it really hurt, he might be a little more cautious at age 14 when his friend suggests they try to ride their bikes across a pipe spanning a rocky riverbed.

We'll come back to all this in a bit more detail in the next chapter.

Computer games

If you haven't already discovered that boys like computers, the internet, computer games and generally anything vaguely gadget-like, then you soon will. Boys of all ages love electronic toys. I'm not even really sure why that is; we just do. I'm sure it's the same as why some women love shoes: they can't explain it in any logical sense; they just do. Let most men loose in an electronics store and they are in boy heaven. In fact just last night my brother-in-law showed me all the cool stuff his new iPhone can do and – trust me – it could do a lot.

'Look at this,' I said to my wife as I waved the phone around and it made Star Wars light-sabre sounds aided by the movement sensors in the phone. 'Is this cool or what?'

She smiled politely, exactly the same way as she does when one of our boys shows her a particularly amazing twig they've just discovered. 'Very nice,' she said.

I don't think she really did think it was very nice. I think she thought it was a bit silly, and she was just being polite because we had company. Of course, there was also that slight inflexion wives sometimes use which makes it very clear to their husbands that there's no way on God's green Earth that the husband is ever going to get one of those for themselves. Bugger.

So if you've got boys, it's a pretty safe bet that gadgets and games are going to be a part of your life, or at least the constant nagging about how they just have to have the latest piece of electronic coolness.

One of the things that many mums worry about is the impact of violent computer games. If you've ever seen any of these games, you'll know what I mean. In one game, the notorious *Grand Theft Auto*, you can shoot police, steal cars and batter prostitutes to death with baseball bats. Charming. Now, while I personally think that particular game is appalling, it can be quite fun to shoot aliens, zombies or even Nazis. The big question is whether or not there is any inherent harm caused by playing computer games. It might well come as no surprise to you by now that, at least in terms of whether playing violent computer games make people more violent, it's possible to spin that story either way. I managed to find research reviews that said there was no relationship between computer games and violence, and research reviews that said there *was* a relationship between computer games and violence. Either way, again it isn't clear-cut or definitive, so don't worry that because your boy is shooting aliens all day he is then going to go out and hurt real people.

Other issues arise from computer games besides violence. One of the principal issues is that some boys seem to become 'addicted' to their computer games. I have seen many mums who are worried – and rightly so – because their sons seem to display no interest in doing anything except sitting in their darkened rooms playing *Halo 3*. The technology has made huge improvements in the past couple of decades, and the games are now completely absorbing.

I myself spent several hours over the course of a week or so shooting Nazis in a fantastic game called *Medal of Honor*, where I got to be a US paratrooper on D-Day. That might not sound like much fun to you, but let me tell you that for a guy it doesn't get much better. At the end of 10 days' playing it, I realised that if I didn't get rid of it I would never do another productive thing in my life. Even then, it took quite an effort of will to ditch the thing, because there was a large part of my brain that simply wanted to keep right on going with the Allied invasion of Europe. I knew it wasn't the real Allied invasion of Europe, but it still felt like I was letting the side down. The point being, of course, that it was hard for me to do that at age 40; if I'd had that game when I was 16, it would have consumed my entire life.

So what can you do? Well, I have some suggestions; some of them obvious, some not.

◊ Don't buy them a gaming console. I'm not buying one for my boys. Ever. I never had one and I didn't die, so I'm optimistic they'll survive as well.

◊ If he does have one, limit the time he's allowed to spend on it, and police the limit ruthlessly.

◊ Tie time on the machine to jobs and/or homework. For every task he completes satisfactorily, he can earn some time playing.

◊ If he goes over his time limit you don't have to remove the whole machine, just remove the power cable or the controller.

◊ If your boy is spending too much time on it, put it away for a month and tell him he's just going to have to find something else to do.

◊ If he is a serious game freak, and spends every waking moment on it, take it out into the backyard and set it on fire. Seriously. He can't use it if it doesn't go. He won't like that very much, but your job is not always to be liked, your job is to make the hard calls and take the flak.

I have to say that I've told several mums to set game consoles on fire, but I know only one who's ever done it. It did cause some sparks – literally and figuratively – but no one died, and her boy did end up spending a lot less time playing computer games. He also didn't talk to her for a while, but at least it was quiet.

It's also worth keeping in mind that even though some computer games are very violent that doesn't mean they're going to drive all our boys into crime and depravity. There has always been a concern that boys are being led astray by the latest trappings of popular culture. At the end of the 19th century, the middle classes became alarmed at the upsurge in publication of Penny Dreadfuls, which included such colourful characters as Varney the Vampire and the bloodthirsty Sweeney Todd. Everyone was worried this stuff would ruin the young by encouraging antisocial and criminal behaviour. It didn't.

http://www ...

And of course there is also now the fantabulous, wonderiffic world wide web. The internet has changed the world in ways we're only just beginning to understand. If nothing else, it levels the playing field and puts the power of mass communication back in our own hands. Not even the voracious Rupert Murdoch could buy the internet, because it is everywhere and nowhere. It doesn't really belong to anyone, so no-one can buy it. It also means that no matter where you live in the world you can take the ideas inside your head and change the world, or make a billion dollars, or create something sad, or funny, or beautiful and share it with the world.

Great.

Of course, there's also the porn, and the weirdo's, and the people in Nigeria trying to get your bank account details.

All of this is why it's quite good to equip yourself with some basic knowledge about the internet. For example, you may not know this but as well as his *actual* life your boy will also, depending on how old he is, have his *online* life as well which can take any one of a number of forms, the most common being social networking sites like Facebook.

The basic concept is that you sign up and you then effectively get a web page where you can put as much personal information as you want for all the world to see. Most kids just put up their favourite bands, TV shows, celebrities and the like, but some kids put far more than is wise. There is also an awful lot of 'chat' that goes on between people. You can become a 'friend' of someone by clicking a button and then you can talk with them by putting comments on their 'wall'.

Some sneaky parents have created fictitious online identities for themselves so they can check up on what their kids are doing online. Some have even asked them sneaky questions to gather valuable information they might not otherwise have got. I would never advocate anyone do this, of course, because it violates the young person's right to privacy. You, on the other hand, might think that the act of placing anything about yourself on the internet means you've voluntarily given up the right to privacy, what with it being the world wide web and all.

I couldn't possibly say.

The big thing about the internet now is that while you used to be able to keep all the family computers in a public place, that isn't really very realistic anymore. Smartphones, wireless and all the other gizmos mean the internet is everywhere. The best advice now seems to be that you treat the internet like any other issue your boy has to deal with: you start talking about it early and frequently.

He needs to think about what he's putting online, what he's looking at, and who he's talking to. His online life needs conversation and guidance just as much as his real world life. The web isn't evil, but it isn't completely benign either. What he makes of it, and how it impacts on him, depends on what he does while he's there.

As with so many things, it's all about guidance.

And not giving your bank account details to the Nigerian 'lawyer' who's acting on behalf of the estate of your long lost millionaire relative.

Friends

It has long been my observation that the way boys and girls think about their friendships is quite different. Girls' friendships are a much more fluid and changeable world. One day you might be the best of friends, and the next you are bitter enemies. With boys, loyalty to friends is hugely important. Boys will have arguments and disagreements to be sure, but their friendships – at least in my experience and observations anyway – tend to remain remarkably stable over their lives. They are certainly much more stable over the early years.

Boys also don't tend to get into a lot of dramas with their friends. If you argue, then you argue, but then that's it. Sometimes you might even come to blows, but then you just move on. A boy's friends are his second family, and it is with his friends that he discovers the world for himself.

Some boys find making friends incredibly easy, but for some it is much harder. If he is shy, or less confident, then he'll find it a harder road making friends.

There are some things you can do to help your Little Guy or Big Guy out if he's having trouble.

◊ Do the obvious and take the initiative by asking his little classmates over after school.

◊ Have 'film nights' where he can ask a couple of his classmates over for DVDs and pizza.

◊ Find something he excels at (such as music, martial arts, sports, art, drama) and help him to gain a sense of confidence through that. I've seen one shy, timid little five-year-old guy turned into a schoolyard cool guy because he took up wrestling. I've also seen another develop a reputation and gain some serious classroom respect as a serious musician by taking up the piano.

◊ When he's a Little Guy, watch him playing with other kids and help him to fine-tune his social skills.

◊ Even though I don't normally advocate this for kids because I think birthday parties have generally got a little extravagant and silly, if your boy is struggling socially, then throw the coolest birthday party you can manage. You don't need to spend a lot of money to do this either. My friend threw a 'fear factor' birthday party where kids got prizes for doing cool, gross stuff like putting a worm on their head or, if they were completely tough, licking it for the grand prize. Gross – but very, very cool.

◊ Again, while not being a big advocate of organised after-school activities (again, because I think it's all got a bit silly), this can be a great way for your boy to meet other kids in a 'safe' and structured way.

◊ If you have friends or family with kids, invite them over as much as possible so your boy can practise and experience social success. The best way to develop confidence is to experience success.

It gets a little more complicated with Young Men, because they aren't really interested in having their mums organise their social calendar. This is where things like computer games can also became a dangerous crutch. It's far easier to live without friends if you never have to think about it because you're always playing computer games. While your options are much more limited with Young Men, there are some things you can do.

◊ Just be there. Let him know he's not alone. You don't need to say it that bluntly, because that will probably embarrass him and make him angry. Instead, you say it just by *being* there.

◊ Encourage any interest in sports, drama, music, bands or anything that gets him out with other kids.

◊ Part-time jobs are also good, not just for money, but for building his confidence socially with other people.

◊ In quiet, well-chosen moments, you could say that one of the things you really respect about him is that he doesn't follow the crowd, that he isn't into being popular just for the sake of it, and that instead he walks his own road. You can tell him that takes real integrity and inner strength and you really respect that.

◊ We've talked about role models, and so you know my views about that stuff, so all I'll say here is that if there are blokes around who can take him out doing blokish stuff, then you should certainly encourage it.

Another fascinating aspect of Young Men is that they will often have girl *friends* who are quite different to *girlfriends*. Boys will tend to talk more to their girl friends about 'emotional stuff' than to their male friends, simply because you can with girls. If your boy has girl friends, then he's very lucky, and you should subtly encourage it.

Basically, boys prize loyalty to their friends very highly, and so it's worth keeping this in mind as you go, because his friends will likely be an important part of his life throughout his entire life.

Alcohol and drugs

Obviously, this is more an issue for Young Men than for Little Guys or Big Guys. Having said that, drugs and alcohol are increasingly becoming an issue with younger and younger children. I've worked with kids as young as seven and eight who've shown up at school stoned. So what can we do?

Here's my standard advice on this subject.

◊ Whenever the opportunity arises (such as related items on television, films or newspapers), talk to him about drugs.

Obviously you don't want to harp on about this stuff, but if the chance presents itself to have a conversation, take it.

◊ It's generally counterproductive to get all preachy, but it is a good thing to tell him about your values and beliefs in relation to drugs.

◊ Make sure that what you're telling him about drugs and alcohol is accurate. If you don't know, get on Google and find out.

◊ Ask him to explain his views on alcohol and drugs.

◊ If he tells you that he is using or has used drugs, then keep calm, and keep talking.

◊ Have conversations about peer pressure, and give him strategies to deal with this stuff – for example, he can say things like – 'I can't, because my mum drug-tests me'.

◊ Most importantly, make sure he understands that whatever happens, he can always come to you for advice.

◊ You can't expect him to take you seriously if he sees you using drugs or getting drunk. So don't.

These are also some *possible* signs that your boy might be using drugs. None of these are definitive, so don't panic if he comes home with bloodshot eyes, for instance, because he might just be tired. Still, these are some things to maybe keep an eye out for.

◊ You find drugs or drug paraphernalia on him, or in his room. If you don't know what this stuff looks like, use Google Image Search and get familiar with it.

◊ You smell it on him (a sneaky thing to do is give him a hug when he gets home after a party, although remember he may have been around drugs but not using them).

◊ Bloodshot eyes, although some teenagers use eye drops to keep their eyes clear.

◊ Staggering, difficulty focusing, slurred speech.

◊ Sudden change in mood or behaviour.

◊ Loss of interest in activities he used to enjoy.

◊ Suddenly changing friends.

◊ Performance at school deteriorates.

◊ Secretive phone calls.

◊ Money or other items going missing at home.

◊ Failing a home drug-test. (These are now available over the internet so that parents can test their kids to see if they are telling the truth.)

What can you do if you suspect there's a problem?

◊ Don't panic. Most of all don't panic, because that almost always ends badly.

◊ Don't go in with all guns blazing. If you do this, he'll most likely just get all indignant and defensive.

◊ Choose a calm, peaceful moment when you have the best chance of engaging him in a conversation.

◊ Be direct about your concerns without being accusatory.
  — *Good opener:* 'I know that you've been using marijuana and so we need to talk about that.'
  — *Not-so-good opener:* 'I know you've been getting stoned, so don't lie to me.'

◊ Listen to him, don't just lecture him. He's more likely to talk if he believes you are interested in hearing what he has to say.

◊ Remember that just as he has rights, so do you. Principally, you have the right to live in a drug-free home.

◊ If he says there's no problem but you think there is, then call someone for help. There will be drug and alcohol treatment centres in the phone book and they are a good place to go for information, advice and support.

There's no magic answer here other than good old-fashioned common sense. You might want to go read my other book *Before Your Teenagers Drive You Crazy, Read This!*, which is reasonably priced, very amusing and contains a whole chapter on the issue of substance abuse and teenagers.

Shameless self-promotion aside, it is worth remembering that the most important thing you need to do if you think there's a problem, or if you find out your boy has been taking drugs, is not to freak out. This is probably going to be one of the key moments in your life when you're going to want to freak out, and sometimes freaking out might be completely justified. The problem is that you just can't, because if you do then you can pretty much guarantee that he'll stop coming to you and telling you about that stuff.

Cars

When I was 15 years old, and having had my driver's license for a little over three months, I was out with a carload of my friends when we decided we'd see if my dad's V8 would 'do the ton', which is a colourful colloquial expression meaning 100 miles per hour. This was an insane thing to think, and even crazier thing to do.

But we did.

I think back to that day now and it gives me the chills. I could have killed them, and myself, and ruined all of our families' lives, but that never crossed my adolescent pin-headed brain at the time.

'You reckon it can do the ton?'

'Yeah.'

Pin-heads, all of us.

So why is it that some boys act like complete idiots in cars?

If you recall from earlier in Chapter 1, when we talked about the boy-ology of young men, I said that they weren't right in the head. In fact there is a particular part of the brain called the prefrontal cortex, which is the bit responsible for evaluating risk and deciding whether or not something is a good idea or not. Neuroscientists call this 'the seat of reason', and it should come as no surprise to learn that the prefrontal cortex is not fully developed until the early twenties. We also know that the 'social reward' centres of teenagers' brains get a bit overheated as well, so they respond much more intensely to the presence of their friends. So we've got a brain that has a lowered ability to evaluate risk, and is more susceptible to peer influence. All of this is why young drivers are so vulnerable. Once a teen learner-driver has two or more friends in the car they are ten times more likely to have an accident. We put young people in powerful motor vehicles at the point in their life when their ability to make sensible decisions about risk is at its lowest ebb.

But wait, there's more, because we also know that teenage drivers have particular issues with three driving skills:

◇ Visual Scanning: the ability to look ahead and scan the road safely and accurately.

◇ Hazard Perception: working out where the dangers are.

◇ Calibration: working out how fast you are going and things like safe following and stopping distances.

Teenagers are particularly bad at visual scanning. When researchers have measured where teenage drivers look the answer is frightening: essentially they look right in front of the bonnet, and if they're following a car they look right at that, and nothing else. Adults, by comparison look all over the road as we scan for possible hazards and dangers.

The good news is that there are some very simple things you can do to help your young man learn to drive safely:

◊ The best people to teach them the essentials of driving are approved driving instructors, and you can find out more about them at www.gov.uk.

◊ Aim for 120 hours of supervised practice in all kinds of conditions and at different times of the day. The first time they drive on a wet rainy night should be with you, not by themselves.

◊ As they drive get them to describe aloud the hazards they can see (e.g. car turning ahead, pedestrian at a crossing, monkey on a unicycle etc.). The simple act of describing what they see outside the window means their visual scanning improves to the same level as an adult. Instead of looking just in front of the bonnet they begin to look all around as they describe what they can see.

◊ Limit their driving with friends as much as you can for as long as you can.

◊ Be wary of advanced driving courses that teach them things like how to control a slide. Often those courses lead to overconfidence rather than safer driving.

◊ Set a zero tolerance for alcohol and drugs.

◊ Keep them in your car as long as you can. . . don't buy them their own.

Most of all remember that driving is a privilege and not a right. If you don't think they're ready, or they can't keep to the limits you set for them, then don't let them drive. This is one of the most dangerous things they will do so make sure you set the clearest limits you can, and give them as much supervised practice as you can.

21

How to be a cool mum

My father used to play with my brother and me in the yard.
Mother would come out and say, 'You're tearing up the grass';
'We're not raising grass,' Dad would reply. 'We're raising boys.'

Harman Killebrew, American baseball player (1936–)

First-off, if you've skipped ahead to this chapter – or, worse still, if you're standing in the bookstore flipping through the book – then you shouldn't be here. Go back. This is dessert, and you should never eat dessert first. Go read your meat and vegetables, drink your milk, and once you've done that then you can come back.

I couldn't leave without giving you this stuff; it just wouldn't have felt right. None of what I'm about to tell you here has been scientifically tested, or if it has it certainly wasn't done by me. This is simply my low-fat guide to being a cool mum. You don't have to do any of this stuff if you don't want to; none of it is compulsory. I can't guarantee that it will work either, because you might do all of this stuff and he still might not think you're cool.

What I can guarantee, though, is that you'll both have a lot of fun if you do some of this stuff. These are not things to be done all the time, because that will be exhausting for you and he will likely grow up completely feral. Instead, these are things for chosen moments. This is not a balanced diet, it's candyfloss. These are potentially golden moments, nothing less and nothing more. These are also just starters. I'm sure you will have many more ideas of your own that are far better.

And a final qualifier is that the intention of these suggestions is not to help you to be his friend, because he doesn't need you to be his friend. He can go find those for himself. He needs you to be his mum. These are just suggestions of little bits and pieces you can do to make him think that his mum is . . . you know . . . cool.

So, broken down into the three stages of boy-ology, let me give you my top tips on how to be a cool mum.

Little Guys

(2–6 years)

These guys are easy. All you really need to do is get out of bed to be a cool mum with Little Guys. That said, there are some things you can sprinkle on top that will make him think you are just the bee's knees.

◊ Every so often, eat dessert first.

◊ When he goes to sit down, make a farty noise and then tell him to say excuse me.

◊ Help him build a hut.

◊ When he's inside the hut, knock it over as you're yelling that you're Hurricane Mum.

◊ Splash in puddles with him.

◊ When you go to the beach for a walk, let him muck about in the water until his clothes are soaking wet.

◊ Watch cool films together and eat popcorn.

◊ Go out for occasional walks after dark.

◊ Teach him wrestling moves. (You can learn these off YouTube.)

◊ Have water fights.

◊ Encourage him to climb high things.

◊ Occasionally buy him sugary, fatty, ridiculous things.

◊ Go to museums and amaze him with stuff you know about dinosaurs. (Google is all you need.)

◊ Make up ridiculous facts at museums. ('Did you know that whales make the loudest farts of any animals? It's just that no one can hear them, because they fart underwater.')

◊ Turn the music up really loud and dance.

◊ Hold him upside-down until he screams.

◊ Chase him round and round the house.

◊ Pick him up and throw him onto the couch. (Care needed here obviously, but Little Guys *love* this.)

◊ Let him help push the lawnmower.

◊ Let him make an extra-big mess in the house from time to time.

◊ Let him play in mud.

◊ If there's no mud, make some for him.

◊ Have sword fights with him. (If you don't have actual swords, rolled-up newspaper is almost as good.)

◊ Have adventures (ie, walks) in the wildest place you can find.

◊ Always remember that a boy's room needs a certain level of chaos and mess to be effective.

◊ Help him build Lego stuff, not all the time, but just when it's fun.

◇ Cover everything in plastic, give him paints and let him get as messy as he can.

◇ Paint a moustache and beard on him. Let him do the same to you.

◇ Laugh long, hard and often.

◇ Tell him dumb jokes.

◇ Sing silly songs.

◇ Call him silly names (things like Jinky Monkey Trousers Jones, or Mungo-bally-mumping Jones).

◇ Give him cuddles and kisses all the time.

Like I said, Little Guys will think you're cool if you just get out of bed in the morning. That won't last forever, though, and sooner or later you're going to have to start working for the accolades. The secret is to be loud, silly and fun. If you can work in anything about farting, then you're made.

Big Guys

(7–11 years)

These are important years in which to stamp your credibility as a cool mum. The distant clouds of the teenage years are beginning to gather, so now is the time to get in and rack up a few points before the next bit hits. The good news is that a lot of the stuff that works with Little Guys also works with Big Guys.

◇ Every so often, eat dessert first.

◇ Give him hammers, nails and saws to build huts with.

◇ Keep up with the farty noises when he sits down.

◇ Puddles are also still good, although you need to watch this one because it can switch from 'fun' to 'babyish' overnight.

◇ Bury him in the sand up to his neck.

◇ Watch cool films and eat popcorn.

◇ More water fights and junk food.

◇ Go to museums and listen to him tell you the amazing things he knows.

◇ Then tell him he's wrong and make up something ridiculous.

◇ Turn the music up really loud and dance.

◇ When he's drying the dishes, let him dry the largest, sharpest knives you have.

◇ Let him push the lawnmower by himself.

◇ Let him make messes around the house from time to time that you wouldn't normally tolerate.

◇ Let his room be *his* room to arrange and re-arrange as often as he wants.

◇ Accept a base level of untidiness in his room as being simply the nature of things.

◇ Help him build model planes, boats or spaceships, if that's his thing.

◇ Build a ramp (all you need is a brick and a two-foot-long piece of wood) so he can do jumps on his bike.

◇ Tell him to go faster.

◇ Let him roam further and further from home on his own.

◇ Get him dangerous presents, like archery sets.

◇ Let him smash stuff from time to time. Any old thing you don't want is fine. Boys love smashing things.

◇ Practise telling him off in 10 words or less, and then moving on.

◇ Ask him what he thinks.

◇ Laugh your arse off as much as you can.

◇ Sing silly songs.

◇ Tell him dumb jokes.

◇ Laugh at his dumb jokes.

◇ Encourage him to do reckless things, like climbing trees that are really high.

◇ Give him cuddles and kisses as often as you can. Try not to do that quite so much at school or when his friends are about.

Essentially the trick with Big Guys, as well as all the silly, noisy, messy stuff, is to let them do more and more dangerous and risky stuff. Let them roam, climb and jump off things as much as you can tolerate. If you believe in their ability to navigate the world – even if you're only faking it sometimes – they will come to believe it themselves, and they'll think you're pretty cool.

Young Men

(12–18 years)

The truth is that there's not much you can do to make your Young Man think you're cool. Part of what he'll be going through at this point is usually thinking that you are a complete nag and totally embarrassing. What you can do, though, is stack the odds so that later on he'll look back on this time in his life and decide that, actually, you were pretty cool after all.

◇ Every so often, eat dessert first.

◇ Don't try to be cool, or to be his friend. It never works, and it's just embarrassing for everyone.

◇ When his friends come over, give them plenty of space to do their 'thing'.

◊ Occasionally play your music really loud, even if he hates your music.

◊ Have your friends over. Sit about, talk and laugh. Having your own life is cool.

◊ If the opportunity presents itself, watch a DVD together and eat popcorn.

◊ If it's possible, and if he'll tolerate it, go on a road trip together somewhere.

◊ One time, when he's done something so catastrophically stupid that he's sure he's going to get the mother-of-all lectures, don't. Instead, nod for a minute and say something to the effect of 'Shit happens. Learn from it. Move on.'

◊ Let him make big decisions.

◊ So long as his room isn't a biohazard, close the door and let him be. Seriously, a clear floor and a made bed is not worth the aggravation.

◊ Every so often, let him go somewhere or do something that he never thought you'd say yes to.

◊ Genuinely ask what he thinks about something, and if he tells you, then genuinely listen.

◊ Cuddle and kiss him whenever you can, even if you have to do it by surprise attack.

◊ Have the wisdom of granite (which is, of course, that things work themselves out in time).

The last point is probably the key one. He's likely to be a bit grumpy and rude during these years, but if you keep your head in the right place, and you have faith that he'll eventually work it out, then that's what he'll remember.

'My mum was pretty cool,' he'll say one day in some future conversation.

'Why? What did she do?'

'I dunno. I guess . . . you know . . . she just kind of always acted like she trusted me.'

You shouldn't trust him *all* the time, but you should trust *him*.

Epilogue
Trouble in Shoe-topia

For a number of complicated reasons, on a hot December afternoon just days before Christmas, I needed cheap shoes that would give me James Bond-like powers. Obviously Shoe-topia was the only place to go. This is not the actual name of the store, but it's what I call it because it's filled with all kinds of shoes at very reasonable prices. It says a lot for the place that I can get excited about it, given my general loathing of shoe stores. It goes without saying that I'd never go there unless I actually *needed* shoes. I'd never have a *recreational* browse, but when I have shoe needs then that is the only place to go so far as I am concerned.

The primary reason I needed cheap shoes was that in a few days' time my wife and I were taking our boys to India on a family holiday. While India is a staggeringly beautiful place, it is also staggeringly filthy in places as well, so my plan was to buy some cheap shoes and bin them at the end.

Complicating matters was the fact that, only a few weeks before, Mumbai had been the scene of a well-executed terrorist attack that had resulted in the deaths of hundreds of people, including tourists. In fact, tourists had been specifically targeted in the attacks. We'd already bought our tickets at that stage, and discovered, thanks to the CNN coverage, that we were taking our sweet little boys for a holiday to a country that – at least in terms of the numbers of people killed by acts of terrorism – was the second most dangerous country on earth after Iraq. Crap.

Still, we'd already bought the tickets so . . . you know.

Needless to say, the criteria for my new pair of shoes now

included not only cheapness but also the ability to run fast and climb over things at speed. In fact, I was prepared to compromise on the price issue if it meant getting shoes that appeared to afford me any James Bond-like abilities.

That particular hot December afternoon I was just about to try on a pair of shoes that looked like they would magically impart on me the ability to catch bullets with my bare hands when trouble walked in the door. It was the noise that got my attention.

'*Jaden!*' the father bellowed.

'*Shut up!*' the boy responded. '*Stop making me angry.*'

I looked up, as did everyone else in the place, and instantly recognised this family as a walking disaster. The father looked like he hadn't had a job in a long time: I based this assumption on his general unkemptness, and the air of decay that seemed to swirl about them all like a cloud of disaffected, buzzing bees. The mother looked like she'd probably grown up in foster homes, and if she hadn't already lost some of her own kids that way, it was only a matter of time. There was a grandfather as well – at least I hoped he was – who for unexplained reasons was wearing a cycle helmet that was far too small for him.

The boy, Jaden – although I'm sure it was probably spelt Jayedon or Jeyyden, or possibly even Jheyydhon – was a poster child for the 'boy crisis'. I could tell from just a casual glance that he was a walking disaster. He was wearing a black T-shirt with a skull on it, dirty jeans, and he had a haircut that looked as if it had been ripped from the head of a dead drummer of a heavy metal rock band.

I watched them storm about the store, opening boxes, tipping the shoes out, trying them on, then simply dumping them to move on to the next pair.

'*Stop it, Jaden!*' his father barked every so often.

'*Just shut up!*' was the inevitable reply. At one point they stood opposite me in the aisle and had a father–son chat.

'*Why the fuck do you always have to be such a shit?*'

'Shut up, Dad.'

'Well if you weren't such a pain in the arse, I could get my fucking shoes.'

'Shut up, Dad. Don't make me angry.'

At this point the father raised his hand as if he was going to slap the boy. Jaden flinched and backed away, muttering: 'Fuck off, ya egg.'

His father didn't slap him, and after a few more minutes of cursing and stomping about, they stormed out of the store, off to God knows where.

Somewhere bleak, that's for sure.

As I watched them leave, it occurred to me that I had just witnessed the central argument of this book in human form: it isn't *all* boys who are in crisis, it is *some* boys.

That particular boy had probably already been diagnosed with ADHD, and was also probably doing very badly in school. He would be a nightmare in class, and would probably be barely literate. Chances are, he wouldn't make it past much more than another year or so in school. After that, there'd be 'special schools', drugs, petty crime and, if he didn't kill himself in a car, eventually prison. He was a saveable boy, but I knew that chances were there would be no one there to save him. One day he would probably storm about some other shoe store with his own dysfunctional son or daughter. And so the circle of life goes on.

It's very easy to be alarmed at the statistics and the rhetoric around the 'boy crisis', but I think we all need to keep in mind that it isn't about what the global averages say, it's really all about how people treat you when you're a little guy buying shoes. With my two boys, I couldn't care less about the big picture when I'm talking with them about their day. I'm far more interested in what's going on with them in their world. The 'average level of reading achievement' has absolutely *nothing* to do with how my son reads. Similarly, when I'm working with a boy and his family, I don't pause for a moment to think about the 'boy crisis' – all I'm interested in is *that* boy and *his* family. I'll leave the politics to the politicians.

Boys aren't the same as girls, we all know that. There are clear and sometimes quite striking differences between how boys and girls think and act. Having said that, it's my view that all this talk of men and women being from different planets, and having drastically different brains, has done mothers no favours. Always try to remember that you share far more things in common with your boy than there are differences.

Similarly, the modern obsession with male role models has left many mums feeling like they are somehow failing their sons if they don't have one on-tap. If you do have a good man who spends time with your boy, then that's great, and I'm sure your boy will appreciate it. But if you don't, then don't get too wound up about it. These things don't *really* matter. He's not going to grow up twisted because he didn't have an Uncle Bob to kick a football with. He can get his man stuff from all over the place, and he can get his role-modelling from you.

My hope is that you'll leave this book with a greater sense of connectedness to your boy and his world, and with the knowledge that it's not as alien as you may have been led to believe. Most of all, though, I hope you leave this book feeling more confident in your job, and more free to enjoy the noisy, messy, mud-splattered wonder of raising a son.

Mums are not bad for boys, and they don't become irrelevant after a certain age.

Mums are mums.

Which is just fine.

Endnotes

Introduction
15 In fact there's an anthropologist R Dale Guthrie (2006). *The Nature of Paleolithic Art.* University of Chicago Press.

Chapter 3
45 In a very amusing Cordelia Fine (2007). *A Mind of Its Own: How Your Brain Distorts and Deceives.* Icon Books.

Chapter 5
60 Lowest for 30 years Biddle, L., Brock, A., Brookes, S., & Gunnell, D. (2008). Suicide rates in young men in England and Wales in the 21st Century: time trend study. British Medical Journal, 336, 539-542.

61 1.4% rise in suicide Ben Barr, David Taylor-Robinson, Alex Scott-Smauel, Martin McKee, and David Stuckler (2012). Suicides associated with the 2008-10 economic recession in England: Time trend analysis. The British Medical Journal, 345, 13. See online at http://www.bmj.com/content/345/bmj.e5142

Chapter 6
66 One of the various rationales Desmond Morris (2007). *The Naked Woman.* St Martin's Press; Steve Biddulph (2006). *Raising Boys.* Finch Books.

Chapter 7
69 Sciencedaily.com published a story University of Exeter. Different roles for mothers and fathers influenced by genetics. Posted on ScienceDaily 4 November 2008. <http://www.sciencedaily.com/releases/2008/11/081103192411.htm>.

Chapter 8
73 Actually, variations on this claim M Liberman (2006). http://www.boston.com/news/globe/ideas/articles/2006/09/24/sex_on_the_brain/.

73 In one of the few studies MR Mehl, S Vazire, N Ramiraz-Esparza, RB

Slatcher, and JW Pennebaker (2007). Are women really more talkative than men? *Science*, 317, 82. Or online via www.sciencemag.org.

73 Well, if you put a baby in a cot http://languagelog.ldc.upenn.edu/nll/?p=261.

75 Statements like that WDS Kilgore, M Oki, and DA Yurgelun-Todd (2001). Sex specific developmental changes in amygdala responses to affective faces. *NeuroReport*, 12, 427–433.

75 Well, aside from http://itre.cis.upenn.edu/~myl/languagelog/archives/003284.html.

76 A lot of very complex arguments http://languagelog.ldc.upenn.edu/nll/?p=171.

79 Sure there is ML Kalbfleisch (2008). Getting to the heart of the brain: using cognitive neuroscience to explore the nature of human ability and performance. *Roeper Review*, 30, 162–170.

80 If neuroscientists are to prevent JT Bruer (2002). Avoiding the pediatrician's error: how neuroscientists can help educators (and themselves). *Nature Neuroscience*, 5, 1031–1033, at 1033.

Chapter 9

85 It was more than a little crushing KM Bishop and D Wahlsten (1997). Sex differences in the human corpus callosum: myth or reality? *Neuroscience & Biobehavioral Reviews*, 21(5), 581–601.

Chapter 10

87 Actually it's even grimmer Frank Spinath, Birgit Spinath and Robert Plomin (2008). The nature and nurture of intelligence and motivation in the origins of sex differences in elementary school achievement. *European Journal of Personality*, 22, 211–229.

90 Differences in brain sizes Lenroot et al (2007). Sexual dimorphism of brain developmental trajectories during childhood and adolescence. *NeuroImage*, 36, 1065–1073, at 1072.

90 If you want to read http://www.boysadrift.com/2007Giedd.pdf.

91 This whole notion Madeliene Arnot and Philip Miles (2005). A reconstruction of the gender agenda: the contradictory gender dimensions in New Labour's educational and economic policy. *Oxford Review of Education*, 31, 173–189.

92 For example, a study of 413 Bruce Carrington, Peter Tymms, and Christine Merrell (2008). Role models, school improvement and the 'gender gap' — do men bring out the best in boys and women bring out the best in girls? *British Educational Research Journal*, 34, 315–327.

92 As another example Grant Driessen (2007). The feminization of primary education: effects of teacher's sex on pupil achievement, attitudes, and behaviour. *Review of Education*, 53, 183–203.

92 In an interesting study Barbara Read (2008). 'The world must stop when I'm talking': gender and power relations in primary teachers' classroom talk. *British Journal of Sociology of Education*, 29, 609–621.

95 There have been a number of studies H Harald Freudenthaler, Birgit Spinath and Aljoscha Neubauer (2008). Predicting school achievement in boys and girls. *European Journal of Personality*, 22, 231–245.

100 Using data from a longitudinal David Share and Phil Silva (2003). Gender bias in IQ discrepancy and post discrepancy definitions of reading disability. *Journal of Reading Disabilities*, 36, 4–14.

101 As I was clicking Muna Hussain and Daniel Millimet (2009). The mythical 'boy crisis'. *Economics of Education Review*, 28, 38–48.

104 While you can find Thomas Spielhofer, Tom Benton and Sandie Schagen (2004). A study of the effects of school size and single-sex education in English schools. *Research Papers in Education*, 19, 133–159.

104 When researchers have done clever Pamela Robinson and Alan Smithers (1999). Should the sexes be separated for secondary education? Comparisons of single-sex and co-educational schools. *Research Papers in Education*, 14, 23–49.

Chapter 11

109 'Look,' I said Janet Shibley Hyde (2005). The gender similarities hypothesis. *American Psychologist*, 60, 581–592.

Chapter 13

132 Let me just give you Avshalom Caspi, Brent Roberts and Rebecca Shiner (2005). Personality development: stability and change. *Annual Reviews of Psychology*, 56, 453–484.

133 It seems that the more David Schmidt, Anu Realo, Martin Voracek and Jüri Allik (2008). Why can't a man be more like a woman?

Sex differences in big five personality traits across 55 cultures. *Journal of Personality and Social Psychology*, 94, 168–182.

135 Among a huge pile Avshalom Caspi, Hona Lee Harrington, Barry Milne, James Amell, Reremoana Theodore and Terrie Moffitt (2003). Children's behavioural styles at age 3 are linked to their adult personality traits at age 26. *Journal of Personality*, 71, 495–514.

Chapter 17

188 In fact Dr Terrie Moffitt Terri E Moffitt (1993). 'Adolescent limited' and 'life course persistent' antisocial behaviour: a developmental taxonomy. *Psychological Review*, 100, 675–701.

189 'They will be biting Terrie E Moffitt and Hona L Harrington (1996). Delinquency: the natural history of antisocial behaviour. In *From Child to Adult: The Dunedin Multidisciplinary Health and Development Study*. Oxford University Press: New Zealand.

Chapter 18

214 In fact, studies have shown Susan Golombok (2004). Solo mothers: quality of parenting and child development. *International Congress Series*, 1266, 256–263.

214 What boys need are *good* Patricia Bricheno and Mary Thornton (2007). Role model, hero, or champion? Children's views regarding role models. *Educational Research*, 49, 383–396.

Chapter 20

241 In a recent study, researchers looked Patricia Tucker (2008). The physical activity levels of preschool-aged children. *Early Childhood Research Quarterly*, 23, 547–558.

245 I managed to find research Christopher John Ferguson (2007). The good, the bad, and the ugly: a meta-analytic review of positive and negative effects of violent video games. *Psychiatric Quarterly*, 78, 309–316; Craig Anderson and Brad Bushman (2001). Effects of violent video games on aggressive behaviour, aggressive cognition, aggressive affect, physiological arousal, and prosocial behaviour: a meta-analytic review of the scientific literature. *Psychological Science*, 5, 353–359.